1,000 Creative Writing Prompts for Seasons: Ideas for Blogs, Scripts, Stories and More

Bryan Cohen

DEDICATION

I dedicate this book to my mom and my dad.
Thanks for all the hayrides.

CONTENTS

FOREWARD

In August 2010, I compiled two years worth of material into a book called *1,000 Creative Writing Prompts: Ideas for Blogs, Scripts, Stories and More*. The material took the form of writing prompts, story starters that can help writers of all ages to turn an idea into a story. I'd written those prompts every now and then while I was working various jobs at offices, coffee shops and eventually, my freelance writing career. Surprisingly, the book of prompts, which was more of a last ditch effort to get me out of debt than an attempt anything substantial, began to take off.

Two years later, I've decided to start writing prompts more often on a variety of subjects. I have the opinion that every aspect of our lives can be mined for creativity. This book and the other ones that I plan to follow it with will help you to start digging.

Personally, I think that's all you need from me to get started, but I love my original introduction from *1,000 Creative Writing Prompts* so much, I've decided to include it here. Take a look for some tips on how to use the book, an idea for a 30 day writing plan and some other tidbits of wisdom.

No matter where you are in the "trying to be a writer" process, I hope that this book helps you to take the next step. Happy writing.

Sincerely,
Bryan Cohen
Author of *1,000 Creative Writing Prompts*
August 2012
http://www.buildcreativewritingideas.com

INTRODUCTION

My name is Bryan Cohen and I want to help you write. I'm the author of a website called Build Creative Writing Ideas and I'm also the author of this book.

I've found that one of the toughest things for a writer to do is to come up with ideas and so I've created *1,000 Creative Writing Prompts: Ideas for Blogs, Scripts, Stories and More* to help writers avoid this dreaded writer's block that I keep hearing about.

A prompt is a jumping off point that helps you to get your brain and pen moving. Some of these prompts are questions, some are scenarios and many of them deal with your own life and memories. When you use a memory or an emotion to write from, it helps you to feel like you aren't starting from scratch. There are thousands of stories already in your brain and many of these prompts are attempts to jog your memory and to use your brain for all it's worth.

I also feel that when you use your memories and your heart for these prompts, the writing ends up coming from a place of great truth. Even if you are writing a fantastical story about a boy and his dog, if it comes from a foundation of honesty, the story will strike a chord with your readers. Successful franchises like *Harry Potter* work for a number of reasons, but I believe the main reason is that we relate to those characters. Creating from truth is the first step to successful writing.

I'm proud to say that these prompts are original and that I've put many, many hours into coming up with them. I've gotten some extremely positive feedback from users of my website and so the creation of this book was the next logical step. I've written a few short essays to help get you started, but you can start writing from the prompts right away if you wish. So…hop to it!

How to Be a Writer

A lot of people feel like they need some kind of permission to be called a writer. Like once they've taken enough classes or once they've published something there is some tribunal that will decree that they are now in fact writers. Others feel as though they're writers even though they've never even made an effort to write more than a short story here and a poem there.

We live in a tough world full of put-downs and negative talk. If someone does not have the will or the ability to achieve his dreams he may feel the desire to kick around the aspirations of other people. We may hear this kind of unproductive negativity from our parents, friends, loved ones and those we mistakenly see as our enemies.

A writer is a person who can see through all this negativity and still feel passionate about writing. A writer wants to write and wants to figure out ways to make writing more a part of his life. There are some writers that are financially successful and others who haven't made a dime, but they are all still writers.

If you say over and over again that you aren't qualified enough to be a writer…you will fulfill your own (kind of boring) prophecy. If you tell yourself that you are a writer and you tell other people this over and over again, the opposite will be true. But how do you know if you're a writer?

If you aren't sure if you qualify as a writer, there is only one thing you need to do.

Write. Just write. Write as much as you can as often as you can. It doesn't matter if you've written anything lately, just start now. If you have an off week, month or year, it doesn't matter because you can start writing again at any time. If you have the desire to write and you can give yourself the permission to have this passion in your life then you are a writer.

This is about the time that the excuses come rolling in:

"I don't have enough time."

"Writing doesn't pay and I'm broke."

"I don't have any motivation."

Solving these problems is as easy as visiting your local library. Hundreds of books have been written about time management, financial management and creating motivation in your life. Continuing to make these excuses and ones like them, with solutions available at any time (for free, no less) is essentially laziness.

Laziness is boring. A life of spending your free time watching television and learning everything you can learn online about celebrities (or the like) is boring. If you even have an inkling of wanting to be a writer, pick up a few books that will leave your excuses in the dust and try working hard to make something of yourself.

My website, Build Creative Writing Ideas has many tips and tricks to improve your motivation and time management, so if you can't get off your butt to visit the library check it out. For those of you who are ready to write, strap yourself in and try a few of these prompts on for size. Happy writing!

How to Write from Prompts

These 1,000 creative writing prompts have been compiled from various ideas that have floated in and out of my head over the last two years. I have made as many as I can very open ended so that the same prompt could be used multiple times over.

The prompts often take the form of a scenario with a question:

"259. You see a little boy wander into the middle of a busy intersection. What do you do?"

There are multiple ways that you could choose to write from this prompt. You could launch into a first person story or explanation:

"I would immediately drop all of my belongings and run to his safety. As I run into traffic, my life would flash before my eyes and I would hope desperately that I could make it to the boy in time to save us both..."

You could make it into a third-person fiction story:

"Derrick and Joey laughed and sipped their drinks. All of a sudden, Joey noticed something out of the corner of his eye.

"What the..."

Joey trailed off as he noticed a young boy trip and fall in the middle of the road. He was all alone. Joey was the only person with enough time to act..."

Or you could transport it into another genre:

"The boy tripped and fell in the middle of the road. The truck struck him with all its force and it quickly shattered into a million pieces. The nearby cars screeched to a halt and stared with their mouths agape at the uninjured boy."

What you write from these prompts could be the start of an entire story or it could just allow you to get a few paragraphs in for the day. You could write a blog post based on what you write, a short story, a poem, a teleplay, a screenplay, a stage play, a novel or anything else that requires putting pen to paper.

These are not assignments by any means. You can write as much or as little as you wish. Run with an idea until you can't think of anything else and then try another one. Write one story from a prompt and then write a completely different story from the same prompt. What you use these prompts for is up to you. If you turn one of these prompts into a million-dollar screenplay (and I hope you do) go off and enjoy yourself, because I will not expect anything from you in the slightest. I created these ideas so that writers could simply write from the heart without having to think too much so go off and make me proud.

If you don't like a prompt, you don't have to write from it. You can also come up with a new prompt based on the prompt you don't like. Seriously, whatever you want to do with this book and these prompts, please feel free to do it. I just want you to write! If you ever have a question about where a prompt came from or what I meant by a particular prompt, feel free to contact me on my site, Build Creative Writing Ideas.

Writing Every Day

One fantastic way to use this book is to write from one prompts every day to keep yourself trained and fresh. Writing every day can be difficult to get started but once you make it a habit it'll be just like flossing (except much less gross).

The method that I like to use to integrate new habits into my life is a method developed by blogger Steve Pavlina called "The 30 Day Plan." One of the mistakes people make when trying to add a habit to their lives is that they think too far down the line wondering, "How could I possibly make this a habit for the rest of my life?"

Steve Pavlina recommends that you look a lot more short term. He likens adding a new habit to installing some software with a free 30 day trial. Try adding a new habit (like writing the prompts) to your routine for just 30 days. Choosing this time constraint allows you to easily block the month off in your calendar and it doesn't feel too overwhelming to just think about four tiny little weeks.

The best thing about "The 30 Day Plan" however is that 30 days is as long as your brain needs to make a task into a habit. You have slowly but surely trained your brain into writing a prompt every single day and now it's already a part of your life. This makes it a much simpler task to keep writing a part of your day.

Find a time of day that you almost always have free. This time should also be a part of the day that you are energized and awake. If you always get home from work tired, you may not want to choose the ten or fifteen minutes right when you return. The time should be specific and consistent. I enjoy writing in the morning after I've gone on a jog and I've had a light breakfast. Another reason I choose the morning is because if something comes up, I have the rest of the day to find time for it.

Set a clear goal for yourself. Some people set a word count per day or set it at one page per day. To start out, you may just want to require only a few sentences per day to get in the swing of things. An example of a clear writing goal is:

"I will write 200 words from a different writing prompt each day at 8 a.m. for 30 days starting August 1st."

Once your goal is set, all you have to do is start. So hop to it and let me know how it goes. Thanks so much for trying out *1,000 Creative Writing Prompts*. I wish you all the writing success in the world.

Sincerely,
Bryan Cohen
Author of *1,000 Creative Writing Prompts*
http://www.BuildCreativeWritingIdeas.com
August 2010

SUMMER

Nature, Activities and Events

Weather and Nature

1. It's the hottest day of the year and all you want to do is sit near the air conditioner and soak up the cool. What do you think it would be like if you didn't have air conditioning in the summer? What would you do to keep cool and why?

2. You've lathered yourself with sunscreen from head to toe to prevent yourself from getting burned. Aside from the sun, what are some things you might need to protect yourself from during the summer and why?

3. Sometimes it gets so hot in an area that people have to conserve their water because of drought conditions. Imagine that there was a drought in your area so you couldn't play in the pool or run through the sprinkler. How would this change your typical summer day and why?

4. Summer is often the host to some wild thunderstorms. Do you enjoy thunderstorms or do they scare you? What do you like or dislike about them? Where would you want to be when a thunderstorm is happening and why?

5. Describe your typical summer outfit. What do you wear from head to toe and why?

6. You have gone on an adventure with your family to discover what animals might be hanging out in the local forest during the summer. What animals do you find and what are they doing? What animal might you find that would be a surprise and why?

7. Depending on where you live, gnats and mosquitoes might be a major issue during the summer. Create a conversation between two insects that are looking for some good skin to munch on. What might they talk about and why?

8. How do you think summer would be different if you were a dog? What about if you were a bumblebee? How about a penguin? Which creature would have the toughest time coping with the heat and why?

9. You have been given the summer job of mowing and tending to your lawn. What sorts of activities might you need to do to keep the lawn in the best shape possible? What would be some of your challenges and why?

10. Would you rather have the scorching heat of the summer or the freezing cold of the winter? What are some of the benefits of each? Which one would you settle on and why?

Activities

11. You and your friends have heard the song of the ice cream man and

you're ready to spend your crumpled five-dollar bill to take the edge off of this summer heat. What item do you buy? What does it look like? How does it make you feel and why?

12. There are many places you can go during the summer, including an air-conditioned building, a nature hiking trail, the beach, and more. Where would you want to spend the bulk of your summer and why? Where would you least want to spend that time and why?

13. Even though the summertime means they're out of school, some people enjoy reading, writing and doing other school-like activities while they're on a break. Why do you think they enjoy learning when they don't have to? Would you want to study outside of school? Why or why not?

14. Imagine that you and your family have just stepped past the gate of the wildest and wettest water park in the nation. What kind of rides would you want to go on first? Which of the rides might frighten you? Which might be your favorite attraction and why?

15. You are skipping across the top of the water on skis as the boat ahead of you pulls you along at a speedy pace. Describe what you see as you quickly speed around the lake. How does it feel to be going so fast?

16. Not everybody is a fan of outdoor activities during the summer. What are some indoor activities you might enjoy during the hottest days of the year and why?

17. As you lay back on your sleeping bag listening to the sounds of nature, you think back on your day of camping with your family. Where might you camp and what kinds of things would you do during the trip? What parts would you enjoy about camping and what would you dislike? Why?

18. Imagine that you and your family have visited a local farmer's market to look at the most local and tasty fruits, vegetables and other foods from around the area. What kinds of local food would you most look forward to trying? If you could grow your own food, what would it be and why?

19. To earn some money for that new bike you've been eyeing, you and your siblings or friends have set up a lemonade stand to serve thirsty customers. What recipe do you use to make your lemonade, how do you price it, and how successful are you at raising funds?

20. One of the best parts of summer is going to see a big blockbuster movie on the big screen at the theater. What kind of movies do you enjoy the most and why? What movie snacks would you eat during the most exciting moments of the movie?

Sports

21. There's nothing like jumping into the pool on a hot summer's day. For some, however, the pool is all about training and doing as many laps as quickly

as possible. What do you do when you're in the pool and why?

22. Imagine that you have been entered into a beach volleyball tournament with a few of your best friends. What skills would you need to successfully compete for the grand prize of $1,000? Would you have a strategy to try to win? Why or why not?

23. You are out on the water at a beautiful beach catching waves with your surfboard. Describe what it might feel like to have the wind whipping against your face as your balance atop a frothy wave in the ocean. What would it look like? Would you be afraid? Why or why not?

24. Imagine that you and your best friend are canoeing down some white water river rapids. What kind of equipment might you need to wear? How would you navigate the treacherous waters? Would it be tough? Why or why not?

25. You have been challenged to a game of backyard horseshoes...by a horse! What do you and the horse talk about during your match? Who is most likely to win and why?

26. Your entire extended family has traveled to the miniature golf course for an intense set of eighteen holes. Which of your family members do you think would be the best at mini golf? What mini golf skills do you think you possess? Would you have a chance of winning? Why or why not?

27. It's match point in a ferocious tennis match with your rival. As you stand there on the blazing hot court with sweat dripping down your face, how do you feel and why? What will you have to do to successfully defeat your opponent?

28. You and your family have embarked on a leisurely bike ride throughout your neighborhood. What are some of the sights you might see during your trip? Where might you all stop for lunch? How would you feel afterward and why?

29. While a lot of people play summer sports, it can be difficult because the temperature can sometimes hit 100 degrees. Which sport do you think is the toughest to play in the heat and why? If you were to play that sport during the hottest day of the year, what precautions would you take and why?

30. During the summer, some kids will go to a camp for a certain sport for an entire week or two. If you had a chance to go to one of these camps, which sport would you choose and why? In what ways do you think you might improve at that particular sport?

Events

31. After weeks of training, you're finally ready to compete in a very summery competition: racing on a block of ice down a hill. Describe the day of the race, how you stack up against the other racers, and what you do in an

effort to win. Are you successful? Why or why not?

32. A common summer event is the backyard barbecue. What is your food of choice during this meat-filled extravaganza? How well do you think you'd do if you were the grillmaster of this patty-flipping party and why?

33. You have been given the choice to pick any outdoor concert in town as a weeknight activity. What is your favorite kind of music and why? What would it be like to see that type of music outdoors and why?

34. The summer is one of the best times to go stargazing with your family. Imagine that you are primed and ready to watch a famous meteor shower with hundreds of other people at a local park. What might you see? How would it make you feel and why?

35. You have been selected as the grand marshal of a summer parade. Why did you receive this honor? What is it like to be the leader of a massive parade of floats and bands? How does it make you feel and why?

36. A Renaissance Fair is an event in which you are transported back to the olden times of the 1500s and surrounded by knights, queens, horses, and full turkey legs. What do you think it would be like for your family to visit such a place during the summer? Who would enjoy it the most and why?

37. The summer is jam-packed with street festivals that serve delicious foods that can include anything from gourmet burgers to specialty ice cream. If you could create a street festival dedicated to one type of food, what would it be and why? Why do you think people would like it?

38. After years of training, you have been hired to fly in the annual air show. What kind of tricks do you include in your plane routine? What does it feel like to have everybody watching you? Would you be afraid? Why or why not?

39. Another type of summer festival can center on arts and crafts. What is your favorite type of art and why do you like it? If you could have an artist personally create any artwork in your room, what would it be and why?

40. Running events like three-mile races occur all year long but tend to be more frequent during the summer. What do you think you'd have to do to train for a three-mile race? Who would run it with you? How well do you think you'd do and why?

A Mixed Bag #1

41. How would summer be different if you lived in the following places and why: the desert, an island, the top of a mountain, and Alaska?

42. What is the strangest thing you've ever seen happen during the summer? Why was it so weird? What might other people have thought about what you saw and why?

43. What is your favorite way to cool down during the summer? How well does it work? Do you think that such a method would work for you when

you're older? Why or why not?

44. Create a made-up story using the following words: beach, Frisbee, crab, and sunscreen.

45. Imagine that you were an Olympic athlete who had to train outside for your events during the hottest days of the summer. How would you keep yourself healthy and safe? What parts of your training would be the most difficult and why?

46. What are some sounds that remind you of the summertime? Would it still feel like summer even if you heard them during another season? Why or why not?

47. You have planned a pool party with all of your best friends. What activities do you have available for all of your guests? What food will you eat? Will it be a success? Why or why not?

48. Would you rather go to sleep-away camp or stay at home during the summer? What are the positives and negatives of either option? Would your parents make the same choice as you? Why or why not?

49. Imagine a summer vacation with every member of your extended family along for the ride. Which family member would you enjoy hanging out with the most? Why? Which ones would you try to avoid and why?

50. While some people look forward to summer vacation, other people wish they could stay in school all year long. What is another example of something that two people might look at completely differently? Do you think it's important for people to have different opinions? Why or why not?

Science and Snacks

Food

51. Describe what it feels like to bite into a juicy slice of watermelon on a hot summer's day. How does it make you feel and why?

52. Your family has given you permission to pick all of the foods you want to cook during a neighborhood barbecue. What foods do you put on the menu and why? How do the guests enjoy your food selection?

53. There are many different sources and varieties of lemonade including lemonade from a mix, in a can, and freshly squeezed. What is your favorite kind of lemonade and why? If you were running a lemonade stand, would you use that kind? Why or why not?

54. Imagine that you have just gotten a new job creating new summer ice cream flavors. What are some of the ideas you might come up with? Which would you enjoy eating the most and why?

55. Eating that corn on the cob didn't start with your parents putting it in

the oven. Trace the steps of where the corn came from, including the grocery store, the farmer, and the people who drove it there. How is the corn's story similar to the stories of other foods you eat?

56. What fresh fruits would you put into a summer fruit smoothie? What benefits might you get from eating so much real fruit? Would you add sugar or anything else to it? Why or why not?

57. Cotton candy is a delicious summer carnival treat, but the candy's texture is so strange it's almost as if the tasty treat is from another planet. Imagine that cotton candy was from outer space. Where would it have come from and how did it get here?

58. Describe a trip through the local farmer's market to buy fresh vegetables and herbs with your family. What do you enjoy about the market and why? What don't you enjoy and why don't you like it?

59. One of the best parts of visiting the local pool or beach is the chance to get what you want from the snack bar. What are some of your favorite snack bar choices? If you had the choice between a tasty snack bar treat or something fresh from the ocean, which would you rather have and why?

60. Different parts of the world have different summer foods, ranging from fried county fair desserts to salty seafood. What would you consider to be a summer delicacy in your area? If you could choose one place in the world to visit just because of the food, where would it be and why?

Animals

61. While floating in the ocean, you see a big jellyfish just a few feet away! What is your next step? What would you do if you got stung and why?

62. Imagine that you are a tiny hummingbird drinking from a feeder in a beautiful garden. What would it be like to fly around so fast? What might be some dangers you would face on a daily basis? Where would you live and why?

63. Upon visiting a desert village, your family has decided to ride camels into town. What might it be like to sit atop this humped creature while moving through the sand? Would you be scared? Why or why not?

64. Summer is a wonderful time to visit the animals at the zoo. Which is your favorite animal to watch while walking through the zoo and why? What would it be like to share a cage with him or her? What would you do together and why?

65. Imagine that all humans had necks as long and tall as those of giraffes. How would our lives be different? What different kinds of clothes might we need to create? Would it be better to have our regular necks or giraffe necks and why?

66. Create a conversation between two tropical birds watching a safari of tourists taking pictures. What might the two birds have to say about the

strange-looking humans and why?

67. There you are at the starting line, ready to race against a cheetah. Do you think you'd stand a chance? Why or why not? Would your chances improve if you had a bike or a car? Why or why not?

68. If you live in a warm enough climate, you likely have gnats and mosquitoes to deal with during the nights of summer. What are some dangers of these insects? What are some of the ways to avoid being bitten?

69. Some kinds of birds and elephants can have a symbiotic relationship, as the birds can get a meal from the back of an elephant and the elephants can be pest free. Do you have a symbiotic relationship with anyone in your life? If so, who is it and how do you benefit each other? If not, imagine life as one of these elephant-friendly birds and write about your day.

70. The animals of summer can be very different from town to town. What are some of summer animals in your area and how do they interact with humans?

Plants

71. Plants like cacti and succulents survive summer by storing the water they take in. Imagine that you looked and acted like a cactus when it came to storing liquid and being prickly. What sorts of things wouldn't you be able to do? What benefits might there be to the cactus lifestyle?

72. Perennials, plants that live for two or more years, may go to sleep during the summer to avoid the scorching temperatures. What would your parents do if you decided not to leave your room or do anything of value all summer long? Would you get bored?

73. You've been challenged to a pepper-eating contest. The person to eat the most summer peppers without drinking water is the winner. Would you take up that challenge? If so, what would your secret weapon be for winning? If not, who that you know might be willing?

74. Certain plants like yarrow flowers, Russian sage, and frostweed, thrive with low amounts of water and might actually die with too much. What does it mean to have too much of a good thing? Has that ever happened to you? If so, explain what occurred, and if not, what might you overindulge in and why?

75. Tomatoes, which are grown during the summer, used to be thrown at performers who told bad jokes back in the nineteenth century. Have you ever seen a show, live or on television, that might have deserved some tomatoes heaved its way? What was so bad about it?

76. To make some extra money over the summer, you've started your own landscaping business. What would it be like to have to cut dozens of lawns every day? What would you think about while riding your mower to pass the time? Would you enjoy the work? Why or why not?

77. Avocados, the primary ingredient in guacamole, are a delicious summer treat despite being green. Have you ever assumed something would taste different because of how it looked on the outside? Do you think the same kind of thing could happen with a person? Why or why not?

78. Your family has moved to the countryside to begin creating grape and berry juices by stomping on the fruits from sunrise to sunset. Describe what it might feel like to squish the grapes and berries underneath your toes. Would you enjoy it? Why or why not?

79. What do the plants in your area smell like? How do they smell different from plants during other seasons and why?

80. Create a conversation between a summer plant and a summer animal. How would they be enjoying the toastiest season and why?

Science

81. The tilting of the Earth gives the Northern Hemisphere its most daytime hours of the entire year. What are some of the ways that you take advantage of having more daylight? What are the pros and cons of having more daylight?

82. A particle of sand that you pick up on the beach could be from thousands of miles away. Imagine the journey of that single grain of sand. How do you think the sand ended up where you might be sitting during your summer vacation?

83. Waves in the ocean can be caused by storms that are thousands of miles away. What are some of the things that you enjoy doing on a summer wave? Would you rather experience waves in a controlled wave pool or in the ocean and why?

84. The largest sand castle in the world was over 30 feet tall and took more than 100 truckloads of sand. Imagine that you and some friends were trying to beat the record. What would your massive castle look like and how would you succeed?

85. Summer is a season full of thunderstorms and lighting. Lightning results from friction in the air and a difference in electrical charge between the sky and the ground. Are you afraid of lightning? Why or why not? Why is it important to be safe during a storm?

86. Coral reefs are important near a tropical island because they keep the waves from damaging the beach. Scientists have created artificial reefs by intentionally sinking ships that the coral and fish can live inside. Do you think a fish would realize it's living inside a boat as opposed to the natural ocean? Why or why not?

87. Sunburns, a summer fixture, are caused when ultraviolet light penetrates through the atmosphere and causes damage to your skin. What are some ways

to prevent sunburn from happening? Why is it important to protect yourself even if you have a tan?

88. Sweat may be a bit gross but it's necessary to keep yourself cool. Think back to the sweatiest you've ever been. What caused you to sweat so much? How did you feel afterwards and why?

89. Ice cream headaches or brain freezes are caused when the nerves above the roof of your mouth get too cold. Have you ever eaten a lot more ice cream than you should? If so, what flavor was it and what happened afterwards? If not, why do you think it's important to eat dessert in moderation?

90. Fireflies are known for lighting up the night sky during the summer. These beetles use the process of bioluminescence to either find a mate or find another firefly they want to eat. If you could light up at night, what would you use your ability for and why?

A Mixed Bag #2

91. What is your most memorable summer experience? Why does this memory stick out so much? What could have made it even more distinct and why?

92. As you get older, what are some of the things you'll be able to do during the summer that you can't do now? Would you want to do those things as soon as possible? Why or why not?

93. Imagine that you could create your perfect backyard pool, full of all the pool games and toys you could ever want. Describe everything about this ideal pool. Why would you enjoy it so much?

94. You have finally made it to the front of the line for the tallest and scariest waterslide in the world. How do you feel as you get ready to jump in? What do you feel like as you speedily propel forward?

95. How would summer be different for the following individuals and why: firefighter, ice cream man, costumed baseball team mascot, and dog?

96. Create a made-up story using the following words: heat wave, air conditioning, bubbly, and laughter.

97. There are many different kinds of summer camps from soccer camp to cooking camp. If you could attend one camp, even an imaginary one, what would it be and why? What would your three favorite activities be there and why?

98. One of the first summer jobs for many teenagers is as a counselor at a camp. Do you think you'd enjoy being a counselor? Why or why not? What would you enjoy the most about leading a bunch of kids through some fun summer games and why?

99. Your family is going on a long summer hike and you've brought dozens of ways to cool you all down if you get too hot. What are the top three things

you've packed to keep yourselves cool? Which one is the best and why?

100. You are a dry blade of grass during the dog days of summer. What kind of things might you be thinking about and why? How would you feel if it started to drizzle and why?

People, Facts and Fun

People

101. You are a lifeguard at the local pool for the summer. Imagine what it would be like to actually have to save someone from drowning. Would you be scared? Why or why not? What might some of your other lifeguard responsibilities be and why?

102. As the operator of an ice cream truck, you provide sugary joy for the kids (and some adults) as you play your high-pitched music up and down the street. What would some of the challenges of the job be? How would making kids happy for a living make you feel and why?

103. The summer is typically the busiest season for a hotel housekeeper. How would it feel to see different families from all over the world enjoying themselves? Would there be any aspects of cleaning up after them that you would like? Why or why not?

104. After going to tech school, you realized that your calling was in making other people cool. Fixing air conditioners is a necessity during the hottest months of the year. How do people typically react to your arrival? Do you feel a sense of pride being able to take apart a complex machine and put it back together? Why or why not?

105. On the hottest days of the summer, your job as a costumed colonial actor is in the most demand. On July 4th and throughout the season, you pretend to be Benjamin Franklin at Colonial Williamsburg. What do you enjoy the most about the gig? What do you enjoy the least? What might your ideal acting gig be and why?

106. Even though your mother said blowing things up would never get you anywhere, here you are, one of the top fireworks designers in the world. What are some of the perks of this explosive occupation? Where would you want to create a fireworks display for July 4th and why?

107. When other people travel, you stay home...in their home. As a professional house sitter, you get to experience the luxury of other people's lives while getting paid to take care of their plants, pets, and goods. What would your ideal house sitting house be like and why? Go into great detail about every room of the "borrowed" house.

108. You've just realized that your job as a summer school teacher has many similarities to having to attend summer school. What are some ways in which

they might be similar? Would you enjoy a teaching career? Why or why not?

109. After working at nearly every booth of the summer carnival this season, you've decided to narrow down your favorite. Which is your favorite booth to work at and why? Which is your least favorite and why?

110. You are a professional referee. If there's a summer sport out there, you've officiated it. What would you enjoy the most about being a referee and why? Which sport would be your favorite to ref?

Facts

111. The summer months of June, July, and August were named by the Romans after the goddess Juno, the ruler Julius Caesar, and Augustus, Caesar's nephew. What would it be like to have something named after you? What would bear your name and why? Would such an honor go to your head? Why or why not?

112. Pesky summer mosquitoes have the ability to find warm-blooded mammals from as much as 100 feet away. What are some of the ways that you avoid mosquitoes during the summer? Why is it important to stay protected? If you could choose to find something from over 100 feet away, what would it be and why?

113. Sculptures and structures made of iron, like the Eiffel Tower, can actually grow significantly in height because of hot temperatures. Imagine that you grew much taller on hot summer days. How would you take advantage of this temporary height and why?

114. To celebrate the summer solstice, the Sioux Tribe would paint their bodies in colors of red, blue, yellow, white, and black to symbolize the longest day of the year. What are some more modern ways that you could celebrate this lengthened day? What would people think of you painted your body a certain color on the summer solstice and why?

115. In the summer of 1922, the Libyan Desert recorded a temperature of 136 degrees Fahrenheit...in the shade! Imagine that you were stuck wandering the desert during such a scorching time. How would you protect yourself from the heat? What items would you bring with you to keep yourself going and why?

116. Summer is a time for weddings, but the largest wedding ever occurred in 1995 when 35,000 couples were married in Seoul, South Korea, with an additional 325,000 couples married via satellite. What would be the benefits of getting married in a huge group? What fun aspects of a wedding might you miss out on by not having an individual ceremony and reception?

117. The largest ice cream sundae ever, created in 1988 in Edmonton, Ontario, included 63 flavors, gallons of toppings, and 54,917 pounds of ice cream altogether. How many of your friends would it take to polish off a dessert like that? How might you all feel after eating the huge sundae? Would

you ever try to break a food world record? Why or why not?

118. In 1816, snow and cold temperatures endured throughout the summer months because of an erupting volcano in the Dutch East Indies. It was called the Year Without Summer. How would your family members react to a year without summer? Which family member would be the most disappointed and why?

119. The Dog Days of Summer got that nickname because of Sirius, the Dog Star, which rose and fell with the sun during the hottest days of the year. What other nicknames might you give to the hottest days of July and August and why? What is your favorite activity to do when it's too hot for most outdoor sports and games? Why?

120. August is the most popular month for both tourism and travel. If you could tour any city in the world during the month of August, where would you choose and why? What are some of the facts you'd most want to learn about during this tour and why?

Festivals

121. The biggest outdoor rodeo in the world can be found during Cheyenne Frontier Days in Wyoming every July. How long do you think you could ride a wild steer before you were tossed off? Do you think you'd make a good professional cowboy or cowgirl? Why or why not?

122. Locations around the United States that once housed famous author Ernest Hemmingway hold festivities on his birthday (July 21), such as the Hemingway Days festival in Key West, Florida. If you became famous, what kind of events would people hold to celebrate your birthday and why? What do you think you'll become famous for?

123. If you like salsa, peppers, and other spicy foods, the Chili Pepper & Salsa Festival in Texas every July is likely the place for you to be. What is the spiciest food you've ever eaten and how did it make you feel? Do you think you'll ever try something spicier? Why or why not?

124. The Burning Man Festival in Nevada brings 50,000 people to the desert to live in a temporary community built on artistic self-expression. What do you think your friends and family would do if you lived away from society in the middle of the desert for a week? What aspects of home would you miss? What might you learn from the experience and why?

125. The tiny town of Spivey's Corner, North Carolina, is the location for the annual Hollerin' Contest, in which people judge the best unique wordless whooping cry in the nation. What are some of the wordless ways that you communicate with other people? If cell phones and the internet were never invented, do you think you'd holler more to get people's attention? Why or why not?

126. The city of Roswell, New Mexico, holds an annual UFO Festival to

celebrate the anniversary of an alleged alien crash landing in the nearby military grounds. Do you believe in alien life? Why or why not? What would you do if an alien landed in your backyard and why?

127. Every July, Gilroy, California, spreads bad breath throughout the area with its annual Gilroy Garlic Festival. If you notice that someone has bad breath, do you usually tell them or keep it to yourself? Would you want someone to tell you if you had garlic breath? What are some of the ways you get rid of pungent breath and why?

128. Also in California is the Northern California Pirate Festival, a celebration of cannons, swordfights, and mermaids. If you were a pirate captain, what would your pirate name be and why? What kinds of treasures would you try to plunder and what would your crew think of your captaining abilities?

129. Every summer, the Taste of Chicago is an event that allows visitors to try foods from over 70 Chicago restaurants all in one place. If you had a bottomless wallet and stomach, what 10 different meals would you try to eat on the same day and why?

130. Cedar City, Utah, hosts an annual summer Shakespeare Festival in which many different plays by the famous bard and other playwrights are put on throughout the season. Imagine that you woke up one day and everyone was speaking in Elizabethan English. Wouldst thou be able to converse in thine own tongue? Wherefore or wherefore not?

Holidays

131. How would your family celebrate Father's Day differently if it was in the dead of winter instead of the beginning of summer? Would your dad enjoy the holiday less or more and why? Would you get him different gifts? Why or why not?

132. Imagine celebrating the 100th birth of our nation in 1876. Before gas-powered grills, chlorinated swimming pools, and refreshing air conditioning, how would you have commemorated Independence Day? How would the rest of your 1876 summer have been different from the present day and why?

133. Ramadan is a religious holiday in which people abstain from eating and drinking from dawn until dusk for an entire month. What challenges would you face in participating in a similar fast during the summer? Would you have to avoid certain activities? Why or why not?

134. The end of summer vacation is often marked by Labor Day weekend. If you had just 24 hours remaining of your summer break, how would you use your time and why? How would this differ from your parents' plan for the day before school and why?

135. Independence Day is a celebration of our nation's freedom. How would your summer be different if you weren't part of a free nation? What

activities might you not be allowed to do and why?

136. Imagine that you could create a holiday called Summer Day that celebrates everything that summer means to you. What would some of your personal Summer Day traditions be and why? How would those practices be different than the Summer Day celebrations your friends might come up with and why?

137. How do you think Father's Day would have been different for your father's father and why? How would it have been different for *his* father and why?

138. If your dad could go on a summer trip anywhere in the world for Father's Day, where would it be and why? What would he say if he received the trip as a surprise? Would you enjoy the trip too? Why or why not?

139. While Labor Day signifies the start of school, in the distant past, some kids would miss out on school in favor of work. Which would you enjoy more, school or work and why? Do you think it's important to have a holiday for people who work hard? Why or why not?

140. Work has changed a lot in the last few decades, with more and more people turning online for employment. Do you think that Labor Day, a holiday originally conceived of for factory workers, should change as well? Why or why not? How will work change in the next few decades and why?

A Mixed Bag #3

141. How did the beach get so sandy? Write a mythical origin story to explain where the sand came from and how and why it ended up at all the beaches.

142. Write a story using the following words: surfer, lemonade, convertible, and sunscreen.

143. Create a conversation between two basketball players playing a sweaty summer game on a steamy blacktop court. Do they have enough energy and hydration to keep going? Why or why not?

144. Craft a poem about a dog jumping into a swimming pool to keep cool. Will it get in trouble for this necessary evil? Why or why not?

145. You are opening a tiny lemonade and homemade ice cream shop a few blocks away from your house. Write down everything that you plan to put on your advertising flyers. How will this information get the customers to your front door?

146. Describe a summer-themed app or computer game that people could play to pass the time. What is the goal of the game? What would make gamers play it over and over again?

147. Write a song about a kid holding an empty ice cream cone after his tasty treat fell onto the ground. How does this unfortunate event make him feel

and why?

148. Create an idea for a television show set during the summer. Where does the story take place, what are the themes of the show, and what would the first episode of the show be about?

149. Write a text message, e-mail, or letter to a friend about your wild and crazy summer vacation. What would be the highlight of the message and why?

150. You've received a message from your future self about the summer after you go to college. What does the summer message say and why? Is it a warning or something else?

The Five Senses

Sights

151. There are many colorful sights that can be seen on a busy summer beach during the day. What are a few that stick out for you the most? Of those exciting sights, which one do you enjoy the most about the beach and why?

152. How do the sights of the summer beach change when the lights go down and nearly everybody goes home? Imagine that you're walking the beach on the night of a full moon. What do you see and how does it make you feel? Would you rather go to the beach during the day or the night and why?

153. If you could go to see any landmark during summer vacation, what would it be and why? Describe how you think the landmark might look in great detail. Other than you, who would appreciate this destination the most and why?

154. What is the ugliest summer vacation spot you and your family have ever gone to? What made it so unappealing? Why did you and your family go there in the first place?

155. Which of the following locations would you most want to see during the summer and why: a baseball field, a theater stage, a mountaintop, or your own room? What are some other places you'd like to see in the summer and why?

156. Which of the following locations would you least want to see during the summer and why: a summer school classroom, the side of a highway for a community service trash pickup, your locked room after getting grounded, or a polluted lake? How would you have ended up in that location?

157. Describe a giant fireworks display in great detail including all of the different colors and shapes formed. Which would you say you enjoy more about fireworks, the sights or the sounds, and why? Would it be strange to watch fireworks without one or the other? Why or why not?

158. Some people want to see fireworks up close and try to set them off on

their own. Why might that be a bad idea without an adult supervisor? What are some other dangerous things that people go to great lengths to see and why are they dangerous?

159. Describe the beautiful sight of a table full of summer barbecue and side dishes. Explain why certain food items look good to you and why others might not.

160. Imagine that you've decided to throw a massive pool party and invite all of your friends. What are the decorations you would use to make sure that everything looks perfect? What would your guests think about the decor and the party in general?

Sounds

161. Describe the sound and feeling of a well-functioning air conditioner. How do your summer activities revolve around places that have air conditioning? What would you do differently during the summer without air conditioning and why?

162. What are some of the other cooling sounds of summer? How do you feel when you hear those sounds and why? Would you react differently if you heard the sounds during a colder season? Why or why not?

163. What are some examples of places that are quieter during the summer? What are a few reasons for these locations to be less noisy? Do you think you'd enjoy visiting any of these quieter places during the peaceful summer? Why or why not?

164. What are a few places that are loud and crowded throughout the summer months? Which of them do you enjoy the most and why? What is your favorite sound there and why?

165. Imagine that you have woken up an hour before your fellow campers at sleep-away camp. What are some sounds you might hear that they'd miss out on? Is having that experience worth the loss of one hour of sleep? Why or why not?

166. How are the sounds of summer different in the country as opposed to the city? What are some possible summer sounds in each? In which place would you rather spend your summer and why?

167. The sun is blazing as you and your friends get ready for a wild summer obstacle course. What are some of the sounds all of you make as you run, sweat, and jump through the different obstacles? Would you earn the roar of the crowd at the end by winning? Why or why not?

168. How do people and things sound different when they're underwater at the pool or the beach? Describe trying to understand someone who is talking to you underwater. Are you able to figure him or her out? Why or why not?

169. Summer is a time for travel, which means you'll be using plains, trains,

and automobiles. As you and your family head to summer vacation, what are some of the sounds you might hear and why? How do you feel when you hear them and why?

170. How do you think summer travel was different before trains, planes, and cars? What would your family have used to get from place to place and how would that travel method sound? What would some of the difficulties be in traveling that way and why?

Smells

171. As you try to convince your family to go to a nearby summer festival, a breeze blows the smells of the celebration your way. What are some of the distinct scents you can pick up? How might you use these aromas to get your family to go? Would the plan work? Why or why not?

172. The summer heat and wind can also cause some locations to smell very bad. What are a few examples of places you would not want to live next to in the summer and why? How would the worst offender of the bunch make you feel and why?

173. How would you compare the smell of an ocean and beach with that of a lake? Which scent do you find more appealing and why? Which location would be most fun to spend a week at and why?

174. How do each of the following wet summer smells makes you feel and why: a community swimming pool, a freshly watered lawn, a car after a car wash, and a wet and furry dog?

175. Describe the barbecue grilling process from beginning to end using only your sense of smell. Which part of the process smells the best to you and why? Do you think grilling will be a big part of your life every summer? Why or why not?

176. How does a big plate of grilled hamburgers and hot dogs smell to you? Do you think your feelings about the food would change if you were a vegetarian? What if you were allergic to hot dogs and hamburgers?

177. It's very important to be protected from the sun all summer long by using sunscreen. Describe what your favorite sunscreen smells like to you. What does the scent of sunscreen remind you of and why?

178. Imagine that you could create a sunscreen with any kind of aroma you wanted. What scent would you choose and why? Would it make you feel different about the object or type of food that the scent from your new sunscreen came from? Why or why not?

179. Summer is a season of sweat. What does the scent of being drenched in sweat remind you of and why? Do you think it's OK to be sweaty during the hottest season of the year? Why or why not?

180. What is your most physical and active summer activity? How does it

make you feel to be moving around in the heat? What are some smells you associate with this activity and why?

Taste & Touch

181. You have bitten into a huge slice of watermelon. Describe how the juicy melon tastes and how the taste makes you feel. What are some events and places the taste of watermelon might make you think of and why?

182. As part of a goofy contest, you must dig into a watermelon with your hands to try to find a clue inside. How does the pink melon feel against your fingers as you burrow through? How do you feel afterwards when you're covered in seeds, melon and juice? Do you like the feeling? Why or why not?

183. Quite accidentally, you've swallowed some pool or ocean water while playing with your friends. How would you describe the taste? What would you most want to eat afterward to try to get the taste out of your mouth and why?

184. After taking a dip in the water and rolling around on the beach, you are completely covered in sand. How does the sand feel on your skin? Where does it feel the strangest and why? What will you do to rid yourself of this sandy outer layer?

185. How would you describe the taste of your favorite summer food? In what situation would you usually eat this seasonal delicacy and why? How do you think a famous chef would make it differently from the way it's normally made for you and why?

186. Imagine that you were the chef putting this meal together. In what ways would you have to get your hands dirty to cook it? How would touching the food feel? What would your cooking difficulties be and why?

187. Summer wouldn't be summer without an ice cream treat to keep the temperature at bay. What flavors and toppings would you include in your ideal ice cream creation? How would all of them taste together? Is there anything that could make your dessert even better? Why or why not?

188. After finishing your ice cream, you realize that it's all over your face and hands. How does the sugary sweet treat feel as it sticks to your skin? What would you do to clean it off? How do you feel differently when it's all cleaned off and why?

189. While they're not meant to be eaten, sometimes we accidentally get a taste of sunscreen or bug spray during the summer. How does the taste of these chemicals make you feel? What is it important to avoid getting too much of these products in your mouth?

190. When you completely avoid sunscreen and bug spray, you end up with a summer sunburn and bug bites. How would you describe the feeling of a sunburn? How would you describe how a bug bite feels? Which would you say is the most irritating and why?

A Mixed Bag #4

191. Summer has a way of bringing the community together. What are some activities during the summer that tend to have a lot of people involved? What is it like seeing all these different people together in the same place?

192. The community must also come together during negative summer occurrences like a drought or a wildfire. What are some ways that people need to function together during a summer crisis? How might you and your family contribute during such an event and why?

193. Summer can be a time for big group trips with a camp or youth group. What is a place you'd enjoy visiting during the summer with a bunch of people? What would you enjoy about having so many people there with you and why?

194. What are some summer destinations that you'd rather go to with a smaller group? Who would you pick to be in this intimate group and why? What are the benefits of having fewer people around and why?

195. Imagine that you were an athlete training all summer to be ready for a fall sport like football, soccer or cross country. Would you try to get any friends or other people you know to help? Why or why not? What would be the most difficult part of the training and why?

196. Aside from athletic achievement, what other goals might you set for yourself in the three months off from school and why? Do you think it's important to know where you're headed or that its better to go with the flow? Why?

197. Imagine that you have joined a garage band with your friends and that you practice every day during the summer. What is your role in the band and what kind of music do you play? How will things change when summer comes to an end and why?

198. Your band has become a huge success and you are going to spend all next summer touring around the country. What would you enjoy the most about seeing all these new cities during the summer and why? What would you miss about your hometown during the summer and why?

199. The members of your school board have approved a resolution that will require all students to go to school all summer long. What would you think about all-year schooling? What are some things you and your family would miss out on if you didn't have three straight months off?

200. You have decided to fight back against the all-year school resolution. Who would you recruit for your team to save the summer and why? What would your team do to try to get the rule repealed and why?

Art, Literature and the World

Literature

201. The poet William Carlos Williams once wrote, "In summer, the song sings itself." If summer were a song, what kind of song would it be and why? Do you think summer is more musical than other seasons? Why or why not?

202. According to playwright Anton Chekhov, "people don't notice whether it's winter or summer when they're happy." Do you agree with him? Why or why not? Would you say that you're happier during summer than other seasons? Why or why not?

203. A character in Lisa Schroder's book *I Heart You, You Haunt Me* says that "books and summertime go together." Do you enjoy it when books are a part of your summer? Why or why not? If you had to choose one book to read during the warmest months, what would it be and why?

204. Author George R.R. Martin said that summer friends melt away while winter friends are the ones that last. Imagine what it would be like if your summer friends met with your winter friends during a party. Would you spend more time with one group over the other? Why or why not?

205. Poet Raymond Duncan said, "A lot of parents pack up their troubles and send them off to summer camp." If you were a parent, do you think you'd enjoy sending your kids to camp for a month or two? Why or why not? What would you do with your spare time?

206. Lucy Maud Montgomery's well-known character Anne once wondered allowed what it would be like to live in a world in which it was always June. How would your life change if it was always June? What sorts of things would you miss out on? What would the benefits be?

207. Summer is often connected with youth in poetry and literature. Why do you think this is? How would summer be different for a younger person and an older person and why?

208. Ralph Waldo Emerson said that "summer will have its flies." What would you say are some of the "flies" of summer, other than actual flies? Do you think the positive aspects of summer outweigh the negative aspects and why?

209. Author and journalist Hal Borland referred to summer as a loan that needs to be repaid in January. Imagine that you could actually borrow extra days of summer now but that it would require you deal with extra days of winter. Would the trade-off be worth it? Why or why not?

210. Poet James Russell Lowell refers to summer as a luxury that everyone can afford. What are some ways in which summer is like a free vacation? Do you think the season is wonderful enough on its own that no additional trips or

expenditures are needed? Why or why not?

Entertainment

211. In Bob Marley's song Sun is Shining, he says that summer makes you want to dance. Has summer ever made you want to move your feet? Why or why not? What kind of dance might summer inspire you to do and why?

212. The video game *Animal Crossing: Wild World* says that "we can't let the sun outshine us! We have to beam, too!" What do you think it means to beam like the sun? Who is someone you know who shines like the sun and why?

213. George Gershwin's song Summertime says, "Summertime, and the living is easy." What are some of the easiest parts of summer living? What are the hardest parts? Would you say that summer living is easier than living in other seasons? Why or why not?

214. Nat King Cole referred to summer as lazy, hazy, and crazy. What are some of summer's best examples of laziness, haziness, and craziness? What are some of the adjectives you'd use to describe the warm season and why?

215. The song Summer Nights from *Grease* recounts the summer relationship of the two main characters with all their friends clamoring to tell them more. Imagine that you had a crazy summer tale to tell. Which of your friends would want to hear as much about it as possible and why? Would you spill the beans? Why or why not?

216. In the movie *Happy Campers*, the character Wichita says that people don't change at summer camp, they simply find out who they are and start to become that person. Would you agree that the summer gives you a chance to figure out who you are? Why or why not? What have you found out so far?

217. The Beach Boys' song *Kokomo* refers to a tropical vacation through the islands of Jamaica, Aruba, Bermuda, and, of course, Kokomo Island. Imagine that you could be on the beach all summer long. What would you do all day long? Would you ever get sick of it? Why or why not?

218. In the movie *Jaws*, the summer vacation on Amity Island is disrupted by the presence of a great white shark. The movie was a major hit. Why do you think a concept that was so scary ended up being so popular? What other scary summer situations do you think could make good movies?

219. Surfing is a popular subject of many summer songs, even inspiring a subculture of surf music such as the song *Wipeout*. Why do you think surfing and music go together? What kind of music would you want playing when you went surfing and why?

220. What is your favorite summer movie or television show and why? What kind of character would you be if you could play a part in that movie or show? Would you enjoy it? Why or why not?

History

221. Iced tea was invented by Richard Blechynden, a tea plantation owner who realized his tea was too hot during the 1904 World's Fair in St. Louis. He added ice and the rest was history. What is your favorite summer beverage and why? If you could invent your own summer drink, what would it be?

222. At the very same World's Fair, the ice cream cone became popular when a stand selling the dessert ran out of dishes and took thin waffle wafers from a nearby Persian food stand. Do you think it's important for different cultures and ideas to come together? Why or why not? What are some things other than ice cream cones that could result from collaboration?

223. Dr. Willis H. Carrier developed the first modern air conditioner in 1902, which was originally meant to keep the paper from drying out at a printing press. Why do you think Carrier first thought of cooling paper before he thought of cooling humans? How do you think people coped with heat prior to air conditioning?

224. In the summer of 2008, Michael Phelps became the first Olympian to win eight gold medals in one Olympic Games. What would it be like to be the best in the world at something? What would be the pros and what would be the cons? If you could pick one thing to be the best at, what would it be and why?

225. At the age of 11, Frank Epperson invented the popsicle in 1905 when he accidentally left some soda and a stirring stick outside overnight. It froze, and over 100 years later, we're still thanking him for the treat. Do you think you could be an inventor? Why or why not? What kind of product would you create and why?

226. In the summer of 1853, head chef George Crum invented the potato chip completely by accident when trying to get back at a guest who kept sending his friend potatoes back to the kitchen. Why do you think accidents and other unintentional actions often create inventions? What is your favorite summer snack food and why?

227. Mary Wollstonecraft Shelley had a dream in the summer of 1816 that later became the story for *Frankenstein*. Have you ever said, done, or written something that you saw in a dream? If so, what was it and how did you use it? If not, what kind of creation do you think you could come up with in a dream and why?

228. Benjamin Franklin conducted many of his experiments with lightning and electricity during the summers between 1747 and 1752, including the famous kite experiment. If you could come up with an experiment to try during the summer, what would it be and why? Would your experiment be as dangerous as Franklin's? Why or why not?

229. July is the top month for ice cream sales and was made into National Ice Cream Month in the 1980s by President Ronald Reagan. Imagine that you have been asked to hold a giant ice cream festival in your town to celebrate the

month. What activities would you have available, what kinds of ice cream would you use and would people enjoy the celebration?

230. Before the 1840s, there was no such thing as summer vacation for schools. Do you think that summer vacation is a positive thing? Why or why not? How would your life be different if you had school all year long and why?

Around the World

231. Woofstock, one of the largest outdoor festivals for dog lovers, takes place every summer in Toronto, Canada. Would you ever take a trip just so your dog could have a good time? Why or why not? What do you think a dog's favorite activity would be during the summer and why?

232. Madrid, Spain plays host to a huge water fight involving over 5,000 people carrying hoses and buckets every year. Describe what it would be like to be a part of such a huge and drenching event. How would you feel and why? Who would you take with you to the event?

233. There are many races held throughout the world during the summer, but none quite like one found in Wales during August. Participants scuba dive while riding a bike through a six-foot deep muddy bog. What strange extreme sport could you create in your own town? Who do you think would win and why?

234. The Chap Olympiad takes place every summer in London and includes events such as moustache wrestling, cucumber sandwich discus and umbrella jousting. What other strange events might you create for such a competition? Would you have fun watching the competition? Why or why not?

235. The tiny town of Buñol, Spain is the site of La Tomatina, a massive tomato-throwing fight on the last Wednesday of August every year. Would your parents enjoy being part of such an event? Why or why not? How well do you think they'd do if they were dropped into the middle of the wet and wild event and why?

236. Each July, South Korea holds the Boryeong Mud Festival replete with mud pools, mud slides and mud skiing. What would your family do if you came up to the front door covered in mud? Would you get in trouble? Why or why not?

237. The World Toe Wrestling Championships are held in Ashbourne, England every June. How do you think you'd train for a toe wrestling contest? Which athlete do you think would have the best shot of winning the competition and why?

238. Multiple cultures celebrate the Summer Solstice by jumping over a small fire for good luck. Why do you think this might not be such a good idea? What might you want to jump over instead and why?

239. The Edinburgh Fringe Festival, the largest arts festival in the world,

includes comedy, dance, theatre, and music performed by people from all around the world. What artistic show would you create and bring to the festival if you could? What would people think of it and why?

240. The Running of the Bulls, held annually in Pamplona, Spain, is one of the most dangerous events in the world. Participants literally run away from six bulls that are released to charge through the streets. Why do you think people would want to be included in this event? Do you know anyone who would do it? Why would they get involved?

A Mixed Bag #5

241. Describe the hottest you've ever been during the summertime. Where were you, what were you doing, and who were you with? How did you beat the heat? How did it feel to be that hot and why?

242. What do you think is the hottest place in the entire world? What precautions might you have to take to keep yourself safe? How and why do you think people choose to live in a place like that?

243. You and your family have discovered a treasure chest of gold on the beach using your trusty metal detector. What happens next? Do you get any special credit for it being your metal detector? Why or why not?

244. Imagine that you've been stranded on a desert island during the hottest part of the year. What will you do to survive? Will you get rescued? Why or why not?

245. You have written and published a best-selling book called *The Secret to Summer*. What is it about? Why do people enjoy it so much? How does your life change after writing a best-seller?

246. If you could take a class to learn one skill during the summer, what would it be and why? How would you incorporate this new skill into your life? What would your friends think and why?

247. Your family has embarked on a 50-mile bike trip to explore everything your city has to offer. What places would you want to go to and why? Would the 50 miles be tough on you? Why or why not?

248. You and some friends have purchased Around the World plane tickets for the summer, allowing you to visit multiple cities in every continent. What places would you most want to visit and why? What would you learn in getting to see so many different cultures and why?

249. Which of the following summer activities would you be most likely to do: relax by the poolside, go fishing, build a sand castle, run a lemonade stand, or read a book series? Why would you make that choice? How does that activity make you feel and why?

250. Create a made-up story using the following words: sandy, crabs, drenched, and mouthwatering.

FALL

Nature, Activities and Events

Nature and Weather

251. Create a conversation between two leaves that are about to fall from a tree. One is scared and the other is excited about the long trip to the ground. What do they talk about and why?

252. As it gets cooler outside, it's important to bundle up, but not as much as winter. How does your fall clothing differ from your winter clothing? How would you feel if you wore as much clothing as in the wintertime all throughout the fall and why?

253. What are some animals and plants you're more likely to see during the fall? If you could hide among them for an entire day, what kind of things do you think you'd see and why?

254. What might an animal think of all the brightly colored trees and fallen leaves during the fall? Would the animal be confused? Scared? Describe the animal's thought process during the seasonal transition.

255. What are some of the smells during fall that make it different from the other three seasons? How do those smells make you feel and why? If someone created a perfume that smelled like fall, would it be the same as smelling it naturally? Why or why not?

256. Imagine that your skin changed color like the leaves during the fall season. Looking through your classroom you'd see people in shades of yellow, red and purple. How would this change your day-to-day life? How would it make you feel and why?

257. Your parents have told you that if you collect 100 acorns and pinecones, they'll award you with a special prize. How do you go about collecting these natural items? Who would you take with you to help? Are you successful? Why or why not?

258. You have been transported several hundred years into the past when your town was nearly all farmland. What kind of crops might you see in the area? How would your fall season change if it was consumed by harvest time? Why?

259. You have been hired by a magical farmer who grows plants that produce Halloween candy. Every day you must put all of the candy into a bucket except for one piece. Do you think you'd be able to hold yourself to just one? Why or why not?

260. One of the most important fall vegetables is corn because so many different products are made from corn. What items might you have to do

without if there was a worldwide corn shortage? How do you think we can stop such a shortage from happening and why?

Activities

261. Imagine that your backyard consisted of an entire mountain of fallen leaves from trees. How would jumping in the leaf pile be different when it was so huge? Would you enjoy it more or less and why?

262. You are the top pumpkin carver in the entire world and you can carve these orange beauties into any shape you want. What would your favorite pumpkin shape be for a jack-o'-lantern and why? What would it be like to tour around carving pumpkins for people?

263. The fall is one of the best times of year to visit a farm for a hayride. What might it be like to be driven around in a hay-filled truck, walk through a pumpkin field and hang out with the farm animals? What would you enjoy about it, and what would you dislike? Why?

264. You've been entered into the Leaf Raking Olympics! You will challenge all of your friends to be the fastest to rake up the backyard pile of leaves. What would it take for you to get a gold medal in this event? What would be the toughest part and why?

265. Not only has your family gone to a pumpkin patch to pick some beautiful pumpkins, but it has decided to pick your favorite size and shape pumpkins! What do you look for in a good pumpkin? What would that pumpkin look and feel like and why?

266. The fall is also a great time for picking apples, peaches, pears, and other fruits at your favorite farm. If you had the choice of how to use these fruits, what would you create with them and why? What if you had to make the food items without any help?

267. It's hard to think of fall without thinking of the Thanksgiving feast. What objects would you include in the meal to make it as fall-themed as possible? How would these fall items taste?

268. Imagine that you worked on a farm and had to create a scarecrow to keep the birds away from your crop. What would you do if the scarecrow started talking to you? Would you be more or less scared than the crows and why?

269. You are creating a fall tree sculpture for your mom before she gets home from work. What materials do you use for the tree and for the leaves? How do you think she'd like your design and why? Where would this fall artwork be displayed in the house?

270. Your family has gathered apples, caramel, and chocolate to make some delicious candy apples. What extra ingredients might you put on your candy apple and why? What might your candy apple look, smell, and taste like?

Sports

271. Millions of people look forward to the fall because they get to watch football season. What is your opinion of football? Would you rather watch football or something else during the weekend and why?

272. Imagine that you have been named the starting quarterback of your school's football team. What would it be like to be the leader of the team's offense and the person everyone talks about? Would it be a lot of pressure? Why or why not?

273. The fall is also the time for cross country, in which athletes can log over 20 miles of running each week to prepare for their three-mile races. How do you think you would enjoy running that much in a week? What would you like and dislike about it and why?

274. If a player from the opposite team falls down in a soccer or field hockey match, it's thought to be sportsmanlike to help that player up. Why do you think sportsmanship and being kind might be important in sports? What's more important: winning or sportsmanship, and why?

275. Imagine that you were a goalie for your soccer team and had to react quickly to all of the balls kicked your way. What kind of things might go through your mind when the opposing team starts to come your way? Do you think you do well at the position? Why or why not?

276. What kind of field do you think would be tougher to play on: a field covered in mud, a field covered in leaves, or a field made completely of sand? Why? What sport would be the most difficult to play on that field and why?

277. While it sometimes gets a bad rap, cheerleading is a difficult sport that combines gymnastics, dancing, and team spirit. Imagine that everyone in your class or family had to be part of a cheerleading team for an entire week. What about the sport would be difficult? What would be fun and why?

278. One of the biggest sports events of the year is the World Series, which is sometimes called the Fall Classic. Imagine that your favorite team was in the series and you had a ticket to every game. What would the experience be like and why?

279. Imagine that you are a huge 300-plus-pound defensive lineman for a professional football team. It is your job to stop the offense from moving the ball forward. What would be the toughest part of the game? What parts of your life would be tough now that you're so big? Why?

280. What fall sport would you be most likely to play with your friends in your backyard? Would these games be competitive or mostly for fun? How often would you play if you had the chance and why?

Events

281. One of the biggest events of the fall is when all the kids head back to

school for a brand new year. Do you enjoy the end of summer vacation and the beginning of the new year? Why or why not?

282. Oktoberfest, a fall festival, celebrates German culture. What are some things you know about other cultures? If you had your pick of festivals and parties from every culture in the world, which one would you choose to attend and why?

283. There are events throughout the country that celebrate everything about the pumpkin, from picking them to firing them through the air with cannons. What about pumpkins do you love the most and why?

284. Many fall carnivals and street festivals include a face painting booth where you can get any design painted onto your face. If there was a face painter right in front of you, what design would you ask for and why? Do you think face painting would be difficult to do? Why or why not?

285. The fall harvest is a major event throughout the farming world. Imagine that your family depended on food and the money earned from it to make a living. How much time and effort would you need to put in to make sure the harvest goes smoothly and why?

286. Going to see a play or musical at the theater can be a fall event for you and your family. What kind of show would you want to see and why? Would it be tough to act or direct a show like that? Why or why not?

287. After visiting a turkey farm, you and your family have opted to adopt a turkey to keep as a pet. How do you think Thanksgiving and the rest of the fall would be different with a turkey to feed instead of a turkey to eat? Why?

288. Some fall events celebrate the changing of the leaf colors by going out into the forest and looking at the beautiful, natural scene. What is it about fall foliage that people find so beautiful? Do you think it's the prettiest part of nature? Why or why not?

289. The fall is filled with blues and jazz music festivals. Have you ever heard blues or jazz music? If so, how did it make you feel and why? If not, imagine that you are attending your first concert of this style of music. Describe what it might be like and how you'd enjoy it.

290. The fall is a time for agriculture and local festivals hold celebrations on everything ranging from avocadoes to pigs. Do you think agriculture is important? Why or why not? How would the world be different if nobody took up farming and all the crops shriveled up?

A Mixed Bag #1

291. What kinds of food would go into a perfect fall meal? What kind of foods wouldn't make the cut and why? How do meals in the fall differ from meals for other seasons? Why?

292. You have been asked to make a fall decoration for the outside of your house. What do you make and why? What materials will you need to use? What will your family members think of your efforts and why?

293. What is your happiest memory that happened during the fall? Why was it so great? Do you think that you'll remember it for the rest of your life? Why or why not?

294. Imagine that dressing up in a costume wasn't just a Halloween tradition but an entire fall season tradition and that every day you needed a different costume. What are five of the costumes you'd pick and why would you pick them? How hard would it be to come up with so many different disguises? Why?

295. Create a conversation between two jack-o'-lanterns on the front stoop of adjacent houses. What would they think about each other and the fall season in general? Why?

296. While playing in a giant leaf pile, you're shocked to find that the leaves have come alive and started singing to you. What songs would this red-, yellow-, and orange-colored chorus sing and why? If they took requests, what songs would you ask them to sing and why?

297. Imagine that during the fall season, leaves weren't the only things to fall. The whole three months would consist of people and things falling over all the time. How would this make life a little more difficult? What would your family do to prepare for the dangerous fall season and why?

298. Create a made-up story using the following words: leaves, dance, hat, and pumpkin.

299. Imagine that you lived inside a cartoon world. How would the falling of the leaves, Halloween, Thanksgiving, and the other parts of the season be different as a cartoon and why?

300. In a lot of poems, fall is depicted as a sort of depressing and sad time. Would you agree? Why or why not? What could these sad poets do to have more fun during the fall season?

Science and Snacks

Food

301. Imagine that you were forced to eat three meals completely made out of pumpkins on the first day of fall. What different kinds of pumpkin foods might you see? Would you get sick of pumpkins by the end? Why or why not?

302. What changes would need to be made if you were having a vegan Thanksgiving meal? Which dishes that you enjoy the most would you have to skip? What are some meat- and dairy-free foods that you might replace them

with and why?

303. Describe what it might feel like to sit on your porch sipping a warm apple cider watching the leaves fall from the trees. How would this feeling be different from relaxing during the other seasons and why?

304. Cinnamon is one of the top spices of the season and can be used on anything from gingersnap cookies to spiced drinks. What are your favorite foods that incorporate cinnamon? Why do you think cinnamon reminds people of fall?

305. After a chilly day of leaf raking, what would be your ideal fall meal to warm you up? Would it be a soup or a stew? A baked lasagna or meatloaf? Explain your meal in great detail using all five senses to relay your experience.

306. The summer can be too hot for the oven, a problem not shared by the breezy and colder fall season. If you could create any oven-baked meal, what ingredients would it contain and why? Do you think it's necessary to follow a recipe when cooking? Why or why not?

307. Imagine that you have been given a choice between eating your family-cooking Thanksgiving meal or one cooked by a professional and famous chef. Would you pick the chef's meal even though you'd miss out on some of your favorite holiday tastes? Whose meal would you choose and why?

308. Which would you rather put on top of your fall meal: butter, gravy, or cranberry sauce and why? Would your parents approve of your hearty topping? Why or why not?

309. Create a conversation between a bowl of sweet potatoes and a bowl of mashed potatoes. What would these distantly related cousins have to talk about and why? Which of the two would you prefer at the dinner table and why?

310. One of the major vegetables foods of fall is the mysterious squash. Imagine that you had to hunt for the origin of this strange delicacy for your dinner table. Where might your adventure take you and why?

Animals

311. You have placed a tracker on an acorn in an effort to find out exactly where your backyard squirrels go during the day. After a squirrel takes the bait, where does it go and why? Are you surprised to find out where the squirrel stashes its goods? Why or why not?

312. Snow geese begin their migration trek of approximately 5,000 miles in the fall, heading from the Arctic Tundra to the American south, east coast and southwest. What would it be like to have to move far away every fall and winter? What would you miss about your hometown during half of the year and why?

313. Birds aren't the only animals that migrate in the fall, as monarch butterflies, humpback whales, and caribou all make the trek to warmer climates.

Imagine that all three of these species made the trip to a warmer climate together. What challenges would they face and why?

314. Animals getting ready to migrate start to change physically in the lead up to their long journey, storing more fat for their distant trips. How do humans change physically in the fall after the toasty summer months? Would they be able to handle a walk or jog as long as the birds can fly during the fall? Why or why not?

315. Imagine that you were a crow getting ready to feast on some crops. All of a sudden, a creepy human-like creature, a scarecrow, has been posted in the middle of the field. What might you think of this straw-stuffed person? Would you avoid the vegetables? Why or why not?

316. After having all summer to hang with your pets, it's sad to leave them for the entire day when heading back to school. If you could take any of your pets with you to school, which ones would they be and why? Would your pet be able to behave itself? Why or why not?

317. While Thanksgiving and football go together, you never expected to see a group of 22 turkeys playing football in your backyard! Describe the fowl football game from the opening kickoff to the final drive. What do the turkeys look like during the competition and why?

318. The fox is often known as a sly and cunning animal. How would you describe the personalities of some other fall animals? Why do you think people try to give human characteristics to animals?

319. After hearing a knock on your window, you open it to find an owl waiting to give you some important life advice. What does the owl tell you? Do you believe the owl? What might happen if you try to put its advice into practice and why?

320. If you could dress up as any animal for Halloween, what would it be and why? Would the animal fit with the fall season? Why or why not?

Plants

321. Imagine that you came upon a pile of leaves that wasn't orange, red, or yellow, but a strange fluorescent blue. What would you do about this glowing pile of leaves and why would you do it?

322. Broccoli can be harvested in the fall after being planted in late summer. Do you enjoy this healthy, green vegetable on its own or do you need to doctor it up with something special? Why do you think many nutritious things don't taste great without some added flavor?

323. Some plants use the length of daylight to figure out if they should be creating flowers or shedding their leaves. If a flowering plant could talk during the fall, what might it say about the changing season in relation to its daily routine and why?

324. Different pumpkin species can grow over 1,700 pounds if they are cared for well by their farmers. What special tricks would you try if you were a pumpkin farmer to get your orange squash to get that big? If you were successful, what would you do with such a huge pumpkin?

325. Fall gourds of all shapes and sizes can be used to decorate the outside and inside of your house. Imagine that you were given 10,000 gourds to really bring the fall spirit to every inch of your home. What would your parents think of your design and why?

326. Visiting a fall pumpkin patch is an exciting time for the whole family. Imagine that all fruits and vegetables grew on the ground in a patch. Which natural delicacies would you and your family go picking and why?

327. Wheat, rye, barley, and other grains can be harvested in the fall or winter. Imagine that you were allergic to wheat and other grains. What foods might you not be able to eat? How do you think you'd replace those foods in your diet?

328. Apples can be used for pie, cider, and many other fall treats. What do you think is the best use of apples and why? Would your family members agree with you? Why or why not?

329. What would it be like if another fruit or vegetable replaced the pumpkin as the supreme symbol of fall? How might some fall traditions change and why?

330. Festivals related to harvesting vegetable, grain, and fruit crops are celebrated throughout the world. Why do you think the harvest is thought to be so important? Do you think that the importance of the harvest will decrease in the future? Why or why not?

Science

331. The green color of leaves is the result of the chemical chlorophyll, which becomes limited during the fall as a result of less sunshine. Imagine that you changed color if you didn't get enough sun. Which seasons might cause you to transform? What color would you change into and why?

332. Without the green chlorophyll, leaves begin to show bright colors as a result of other chemicals called carotenoids and anthocyanins. What is your favorite fall leaf color and why? Would you paint your house or room that color? Why or why not?

333. Trees use this season to suck up the last bit of sugar and other nutrients from their leaves before they fall off. Have you ever licked the bottom of a bowl or cup to enjoy the last bit of food or drink? What might your parents think of your manners if you did and why?

334. Plants are also able to put some of their waste products into leaves, effectively taking out the trash by dumping the leaves during the fall. While it's

OK for trees to drop their trash, why is it important for you to humans to pick up after themselves? What are some examples of trash you've seen that haven't been properly thrown away?

335. Another reason for trees to get rid of their leaves is for the plant to conserve its water during the upcoming dry winter. Why might it be important for humans to conserve water? What are some ways that you can conserve water in your house?

336. Not all trees lose their leaves during the fall. Evergreens keep their small, sharp needles all year round. Imagine how you'd feel if everyone around you was changing while you stayed exactly the same. Would you try to fit in? Why or why not?

337. Fall is host to one of the biggest meteor showers of the year with the November Leonids. Create a conversation between two meteors shooting across the sky looking down at your and your family during the shower. What might these comet dust particles have to say about you and why?

338. Flu season begins during the fall and scientists use chicken eggs to create the vaccines against the infectious viral disease. Do you think it's necessary to protect yourself against the flu virus? Would your parents agree with you? Why or why not?

339. The harvest moon is the name given to the final full moon before the fall season officially begins. This moon gives farmers the opportunity to work through the night to harvest their crops. What are some ways in which a full moon could help you during the night?

340. Imagine that humans had leaves instead of hair. How would you style your bushy head and what colors would your leaves change into during the fall? What would you do during the winter without any hair or leaves and why?

A Mixed Bag #2

341. As the season of Halloween, fall can be quite frightening. What is the most scared you've ever been? What caused it and how did you overcome your fear?

342. How do you think your fears will change as you get older? Will you be afraid of more or fewer things and why?

343. What are some of the sounds of fall? Why aren't these noises usually found during the summer or spring? How do these sounds make you feel when you hear them and why?

344. You have been hired to write and direct a Hollywood movie centered on fall and people falling in love. Who would star in it, where would you film it, and how successful do you think it would be?

345. You and your family are hosting a foreign exchange student who comes from a hot climate that doesn't experience much fall weather. What

would it be like for him to see the leaves falling for the first time and why? Would he enjoy it? Why or why not?

346. What would fall be like if we lived in a world without trees and falling leaves? What else might be different about this strange world and why?

347. While trees have no more use for leaves in the fall, there are plenty of things that we can use them for. What are some uses for leaves to lighten your raking load? Which is your favorite use and why?

348. After a delivery mistake, there are 1,000 pumpkins sitting in your front yard. How will you and your family deal with all these pumpkins? Would you ever get sick of endless pumpkin pies and cheesecakes? Why or why not?

349. Imagine that every day of fall included a feast as big as Thanksgiving. What would happen to the fitness level of your family? Which Thanksgiving foods would you get sick of and why?

350. You have been handed a treasure map to the greatest fall treasure of all: a secret stash of the tastiest Thanksgiving recipes in existence. Who will you enlist to help you find the treasure? Describe your journey from beginning to end.

People, Facts and Fun

Holidays

351. Halloween is a time for silly costumes and disguises. Imagine that you actually tried to be someone else for a day. What might your reasoning be for not being yourself? Would you be able to fool anybody? Why or why not?

352. During the time of Christopher Columbus, there were plenty of places left to be discovered. What are some careers nowadays that would still allow you to make a discovery (even if it isn't a new continent)? Which of those careers would you enjoy the most and why?

353. Thanksgiving is about eating food and giving thanks. What are some of the things you have to be thankful for this fall? What aspects of the season are you the most grateful for and why?

354. Every fall, we recognize the acts of bravery and heroism of our Armed Forces during Veterans Day. If you had to be away in a foreign country during Halloween, Thanksgiving, and the rest of the fall, what would you miss the most and why? Would it be worth it to serve as a protector of the nation? Why or why not?

355. While it's not often a holiday we celebrate, Election Day is a day the citizens of this nation use to select our representatives in the government. If you ran for President of the United States, what would be some of the things you'd promise as part of your platform? Do you think you'd have a good shot

of winning? Why or why not?

356. A group of ghosts, ghouls, and witches have arrived at your door and all they want is a meal of all their fall favorites: turkey, apple cider and pumpkin pie. What do you all talk about as you sit around the table and eat? Which ghastly creature has the scariest story to tell and why?

357. You are a part of Christopher Columbus's famous crew during the first voyage to the West Indies. Describe what it might be like to spend several years away from home in search of glorious, new lands. What would you get homesick about and why?

358. What different foods would you eat during Thanksgiving if the holiday was in the summer and why? What are some of the aspects of Thanksgiving that fit perfectly with the fall and why?

359. At any given moment, there are thousands of people training to be a part of the Armed Forces. Would you ever consider a career with the Army, Navy, Air Force, or another branch of the military? Why or why not? Would any of your family members be more likely than you and why?

360. When Congress wants to pass a law, a certain amount of people need to agree on the bill before it can pass. What are some of the difficulties in getting other people to agree with you? If you had an idea for a law, do you think you'd be able to compromise with the ideas of the other party? Why or why not?

People

361. You run the top costume shop in town and every fall there are thousands of kids who look to you to get them the best Halloween outfit. What are your top three sellers and why? What part of the business do you enjoy the most and why?

362. For three years running, you've won first place in the annual biggest pumpkin growing competition, making your farm one of the top fall tourist attractions. What was it that made you decide to go into pumpkin farming? How are you able to successfully grow such huge orange fruits every single year?

363. It's tough being an actual witch during the fall, because there are so many imposters out there, especially on Halloween. What are some of the spells that you cast in your day-to-day life? Is it hard keeping your witchy identity a secret? Why or why not?

364. As the principal for a huge elementary school, you try your best to learn all the students' names and how you can best help them to succeed from the fall through the start of the summer. What are some of your responsibilities as the head of the school? What would you enjoy the most about the job and why?

365. If a homeowner has a leaf catastrophe in his or her backyard, you are the person who can make the yard spotless in under 24 hours. Armed with a team of leaf-blowing and rake-wielding employees, you know exactly how to handle any leaf-related situation. What would you do if a landscaping competitor came into town and tried to take your business and why?

366. You've cooked for 500 and you've cooked for five, but every Thanksgiving meal you've made has made you feel just as fulfilled. What is your favorite part of being a professional Thanksgiving chef and why? Which is your favorite dish or dessert to make and why?

367. Ever since you were placed in the middle of a corn field, you wondered if you got into the right line of work. You've failed to succeed in the first rule of being a scarecrow: scaring crows away. Describe your typical day from beginning to end, including any conversations you have with the non-frightened birds.

368. You prepare all spring and summer for your fall career as a professional football coach. You have football plays to plan and egos to deal with, but you love every minute of it. What is the toughest part of dealing with multi-millionaire athletes every day? What is your best quality as a coach and why?

369. Your job is on the line every fall as you wait to see how well the television shows you've chosen do in the new television schedule. You've been told that if you don't move up from last place in the ratings to second place, you'll be canned. What are some of the shows you've selected to be ratings winners? What is the toughest part of your job and why?

370. You wanted to sell the rundown, old house, but as part of a will, you had to continue to run the haunted house business in the creepy former mansion. After growing up there, you'd gotten tired of cheap thrills and fake monsters. What will you do to keep the business going and to keep it interesting for yourself? What is the scariest part of the haunted house and why?

Facts

371. During its fall migration, the Bar-Headed Goose can fly as high as 28,000 feet to go over the Himalayas. Describe what the view of the mountain range might look like from that high up. What would it feel like to be that high in the air? Would you enjoy it? Why or why not?

372. An acre of trees, which can look breathtaking during the fall season, uses approximately 5,880 pounds of carbon dioxide and gives off 4,280 pounds of oxygen every year. Why is this important to humans and the earth? How long do you think it would take you to plant an acre of trees? Would that time be worth it? Why or why not?

373. American Indians grew gourds like the pumpkin as long ago as 5500 B.C.E. How difficult might it have been to make a pumpkin pie back then? How would you gather all of the ingredients and bake the dessert? What would the natives think about your creation and why?

374. The first Thanksgiving feast is thought to have lasted three full days. What would your household be like if you ate for three entire days during Thanksgiving? Would you get sick of all the food or enjoy having everybody stuff themselves silly and why?

375. When the French adopted a calendar called the French Republican Calendar in the late 18th and early 19th centuries, the autumnal equinox became New Year's Day. Would your New Year's celebration be different if it was at the start of fall instead of a week into winter? Would you take part in different activities during the holiday? Why or why not?

376. The autumnal equinox is a national holiday in Japan. How would you spend the first day of fall if your entire family had the day off from school and work? If you took a fall vacation, where would the destination be and why?

377. An Indian summer is a term used to describe unseasonably warm weather that can occur in October or November. This term is different in different cultures and can be translated into phrases such as "a tiger in autumn" in Chinese, "a summer of old ladies" in Lithuania, and "a golden summer" in Germany. If you could come up with a funny phrase for this time period, what would it be and why?

378. You can tell if a season is going to be particularly cold if you see more acorns on the ground than usual in the fall. This means that squirrels are gathering extra nuts to prepare for the chilly winter. How do you think these squirrels are able to predict the future weather? Create a conversation with a squirrel about the upcoming weather.

379. The planet Neptune was discovered during the fall of 1846. Imagine that you have discovered a planet and can name it anything you want. What would you name it and why? If you visited the planet, what would it be like to live on and why?

380. The first game of the first World Series was played in 1903. What would it have been like to watch a game from the stands of a baseball park over 100 years ago? Would you enjoy it more or less than watching a game in the present day and why?

Festivals

381. Evansville, Indiana, hosts the West Side Nut Club's Fall Festival every October and features strange food such as alligator-on-a-stick, deep fried dandelions, and elk jerky. Create the strangest food idea you can think of as if it were a pitch to the festival. Do you think they'd accept it? Why or why not?

382. Every November, science nerds and normal folks alike shoot

pumpkins through the air with specially designed cannons during the World Championship Punkin' Chunkin' in Nassau, Delaware. What would you use to create a pumpkin-shooting device? Would you need any help to put it together? Why or why not?

383. Abbeville, Louisiana, is the site for the Giant Omelette Celebration, which uses 5,000 eggs and a 12-foot skillet to create a massively delightful brunch item. If you could cook a giant food item, what would it be and why? Would you eat the entire thing yourself or share it with people in need? Why or why not?

384. If worm racing is your favorite hobby, you'll love the Wooly Worm Festival in Banner Elk, North Carolina, every October. Imagine that you were a worm training for this prestigious event. What kind of worm exercises would you do? Would you get some worm satisfaction from your victory? Why or why not?

385. The Stormy Weather Arts Festival in Cannon Beach, Oregon features multiple art competitions including a So You Think You Can Paint Competition and The Quick Draw. Do you think that anyone can become an artist or that it's something you're born with? What would it take for you to gain artistic skills and why?

386. The Big Pig Jig is a barbecue contest in Vienna, Georgia, that started when a group of self-made gourmets decided to hold a contest to see who could cook the best pig. What are some of the skills that a chef might need to win a competition like this? Would you be more interested in cooking or eating the barbecue and why?

387. In the fall of 1971, a man named D.B. Cooper hijacked a jet, collected $200,000 in ransom money, and parachuted into the state of Washington, never to be found again. Ariel, Washington holds a festival in his honor as the only unsolved hijacking in the history of the U.S. What do you think happened to D.B. Cooper and all of that money? Is that a likely outcome? Why or why not?

388. Most fall festivals are extremely loud. The Quiet Festival in Ocean City, New Jersey, is not one of them, featuring mimes, silent movies, and a sign-language choir. Do you think silence is powerful or boring, and why? How would you feel if you had to be silent for an entire week?

389. Every November in Hawaii, the Ultraman World Championships test who can swim 6.2 miles, bike 261.4 miles, and run 52.4 miles all together the fastest. Who that you know would be most likely to compete in this at some point in their lives? What kind of training would they have to do to prepare and why?

390. If you love beans and racing outhouses through the streets, your fall festival of choice might be the Bean Fest and Great Championship Outhouse Race in Mountain View, Arkansas. If you could come up with your own wacky

local fall festival, what would it be called and why? How hard do you think it would be to set up an entire festival and why?

A Mixed Bag #3

391. How did squirrels decide that acorns were their favorite food? Create a mythical origin story to explain how squirrels realized that acorns were the best for them.

392. Create a story using the following words: maple, pile, celebration, and chores.

393. Create a conversation between two old rakes in a garage telling a story about when the first leaf blower came to town. Are they bitter or happy to retire and why?

394. Come up with a poem about a jack-o'-lantern whose candle has gone out while his creators are out of town for the weekend. How does this make him feel and why?

395. You have gone into the pumpkin farming business and you need to write a script for your first television commercial. What do you say during the commercial to get people to choose your farm over other pumpkin farms and why?

396. Your game programmer friend has asked you to come up with an idea for a fall-themed game or app. What is the idea you would have and why? Would you enjoy playing it yourself? Why or why not?

397. Write a song about a Halloween costume contest and a boy wearing a sheet who hopes he can win. Will they boy win and how does he feel after the outcome?

398. You have been hired to create a cartoon set during the fall. What age group would it be for, who would the characters be, and what would happen in the plot and why?

399. Write a letter to your pen pal in another country about how fun your fall has been so far. What is your favorite fall activity to write about and why? Do you mention your family at all? Why or why not?

400. Due to a rip in the space-time continuum, you've received a message about the fall from your great-great grandson. How will the fall be different over 50 years in the future? Does the message say anything about future you? Why or why not?

The Five Senses

Sights

401. What is your first thought when you see a bunch of fall leaves gathered in your backyard? Is it a positive or a negative thought and why? Would the

other members of your family feel the same way? Why or why not?

402. How might a bird or a squirrel feel upon seeing the leaves fall to the ground and why? What might their first action be to prepare for the changing of the seasons and why?

403. How would you react if you saw an actual ghost on Halloween? Would you say anything to the ghost and, if so, what and why? Would other people be able to see the ghost, too? Why or why not?

404. Do you believe in ghosts? Why or why not? Have you seen anything in your life that might lead you to believe in things we can't explain? Why or why not?

405. What is the most interesting pumpkin you've ever seen in your life? What was it that made it so unique: the shape, the size, the color or something else entirely? What do you think happened to that pumpkin and why?

406. Whether it be because of pumpkin assault or decay, pumpkins don't last forever. How does it make you feel when you see a smashed or rotten pumpkin and why? How might the pumpkin feel itself and why?

407. What are some of the sights of fall that make you truly feel that fall has arrived? Are you glad when you see them? Why or why not? What does the arrival of fall mean to you?

408. What are some sights you might see that clue you into the end of fall? How does seeing the end of fall before your eyes make you feel and why? What does the departure of fall mean to you and why?

409. If you could choose any place in the world that you'd have to see at least once every fall for the rest of your life, where would it be and why? What sorts of things would you do there and how would those things change as you get older?

410. Artistic people tend to see fall as a time of sadness, but how do you see it? Do you think fall should be connected with any type of emotion? Why or why not?

Sounds

411. Describe the sound of your feet coming crashing down on a pile of leaves. What does that series of crinkles and crunches make you think of and why? Does it remind you of any sounds that other things make? Why or why not?

412. If a leaf could make a sound like an animal, what sound would it make and why? What would some other fall plants and vegetables sound like? How would fall be different with barking leaves and hissing pumpkins and why?

413. If you could pick a song to listen to during the fall, what would it be and why? In what ways does the song make you think of the season and why? Would your family members agree with you? Why or why not?

414. Which musical instruments or styles of music make you think of fall the most and why? Describe what a fall concert of only these instruments and styles might be like. Would you enjoy it? Why or why not?

415. What are some spooky fall sounds that you might associate with Halloween? How do those sounds make you feel and why? Which one would scare you the most and why?

416. What is it about being in the dark that makes noises, especially creepy Halloween noises, even scarier? What noise do you think would scare you the most if you were sitting in a pitch-black room and why?

417. The sights, smells, and tastes of Thanksgiving are so prevalent, it's hard to remember the sounds. What are some of the sounds that occur around your holiday table? Which sound do you enjoy the most, which do you enjoy the least, and why?

418. What sounds do your family members make while actually eating the Thanksgiving meal? Would you say your family members have good table manners? Why or why not? Are your table manners near the top, near the bottom or somewhere in the middle compared to the rest of your family and why?

419. What are some of the sounds that the animals of fall make? How might these sounds be related to their survival? Do any of their sounds scare you? Why or why not?

420. What are a few sounds that humans make during the fall? Are these sounds related to fun or survival and why? Which of these sounds would you consider to be the most important for people and why?

Smells

421. Describe the smell of a freshly baked pumpkin pie right out of the oven. How does the aroma make you feel, knowing that in a few short minutes you'll be able to eat it? How would your feeling change if there were many different kinds of pies fresh out of the oven and why?

422. Would you feel any differently if you were a bird perched on the windowsill hoping to get a nibble of that tasty-smelling pie? What would you and your bird friends do to try to get your wings on that dessert? Would you be successful? Why or why not?

423. The fall is a season of pungent spices. What are some of your favorite herb and spice smells during the fall and why? What spice-related memories might smelling the spices conjure up and why?

424. Even with spices, there can be too much of a good thing. How might you feel if you accidentally inhaled way too much cinnamon, cloves, or another spice? What other smells in your life have you taken in too much of and what

did you do to correct the problem?

425. Would you say the fall air in your town smells differently than it does during the other seasons? If so, how would you describe the difference? Aside from being a different temperature, how does the season *feel* different and why?

426. What are some of the grossest, most pungent odors you can think of connected with the fall? Which one is the most disgusting and why? What would you do if your room intensely smelled like that odor for some reason?

427. Describe all the smells you can remember from your most recent Thanksgiving dinner. Which one sticks out the most and why? If you could smell any scent from that dinner frequently throughout the year, which one would it be and why?

428. What is a smell that you think could ruin your Thanksgiving dinner? What would your family do to find a way around it and why? Which of your family members would be the most likely to complain about it?

429. What is the first smell you can ever remember from the fall season? Why do you think it's stuck with you for all these years? What other things happened in connection with that smell and how does the smell make you feel?

430. What is the most recent fall smell that really connected with you? Was it a positive or a negative smell and why? Do you think the scent would have connected with someone else too? Why or why not?

Taste & Touch

431. How does the taste of the first Halloween candy of the night taste differently from the last candy of the night? Why might the two taste different from each other even if they're the same type of candy? How much candy would you say is too much candy and why?

432. Eating some Halloween candies is a very tactile experience. Describe unwrapping several different kinds of candy and what goes into actually getting to the tasty treat itself. Which kind of candy do you most enjoy tearing into and why: a foil wrapper, a plastic wrapper, a paper wrapper, a paper package to tear into, or something else entirely?

433. Of all the Thanksgiving meals you've eaten, would you say one ranks the highest as far as taste is concerned? Why or why not? Of the cooks in your Thanksgiving kitchen, who is the best cook and why? What tips might you take from him or her to become a good cook on your own someday and why?

434. Imagine you had multiple Thanksgiving dishes lined up next to each other just to feel what it was like to touch them. The dishes include gravy, stuffing, Jell-O, and at least two others. Describe what each of them feels like on your hands. Which one might be the strangest sensation and why?

435. Describe the taste of a warm, spiced apple cider. Try to identify the different parts of the taste, such as what might be coming from the apples and

what might be from other sources. How do you think the people who create the cider figure out their own blend of apples and spices?

436. To make a little extra money, you are helping out at the local apple orchard as a picker. How would you describe how the different kinds of apples feel as you pull them down? Is there a difference between picking apples for fun and picking apples as a job? Why or why not?

437. What are some of the food staples for breakfast, lunch, and dinner in your house during the fall? Are there any that you look forward to the rest of the year? Why or why not? Describe which meal tastes the best and why. How is that taste distinct from other foods and why?

438. Describe the difference your hands would feel from crumpling up a handful of wet leaves versus crumpling up a handful of dry leaves. What happens to the leaves and why? How do your hands feel after crushing both? Which would you rather dive into and why: a pile of wet leaves or a pile of dry leaves?

439. If you were a squirrel, you'd have a completely different diet from the one you have as a human. You'd eat nuts if you could find them and rummage through the trash if you couldn't. How do you think a squirrel's sense of taste differs from yours? In what ways are you more picky than a squirrel when it comes to what you'll eat and why?

440. Squirrels have the amazing ability to climb up trees and jump from branch to branch. If you were a squirrel, how do you think it would feel to grip the branches as you ran and leapt? What would your parents say if they saw you trying to run up a tree like a squirrel?

A Mixed Bag #4

441. How would you describe fall in your town? Is it a time for people to come together, a season in which people tend to keep to themselves, or something else entirely? How do you think your town has changed for the fall season in the last 50 years and why?

442. What would you say makes your town unique during the fall and why? How is your town similar to other areas in the fall and why? Which would you say is your town's most unique season and why?

443. Imagine that you are going trick-or-treating with a large group of families and friends. Who are the most likely people to be in that group and why? What would you differently with that group than you would if it was just you and your parents and why?

444. What costumes might your group members wear and why? Describe what outfits these friends and family members might wear based on their preferences and personalities.

445. You and your friends have been turned into a pile of leaves! What will

you do to get out of this situation before you all get raked?

446. How do you think trees feel when they lose their leaves? Imagine that a bare tree began talking to you about the season. What would it say and why?

447. If you could cast a bunch of famous actors and celebrities to play your family members for one Thanksgiving, who would they be and why? How would the holiday be different with people *playing* your family as opposed to actually being your family? Why?

448. If your family was replaced by actors for one year's Thanksgiving, what would you miss the most about them and why? Why is it important to be with your *actual* family for turkey day?

449. Imagine that you had no phone or games to play while you were sitting outside in a forest full of red, purple, and yellow leaves. Are you more likely to appreciate the beauty of the season or be bored? Why? How does fall nature make you feel and why?

450. Which of your family members other than you is most likely to appreciate fall nature and why? What is it about this person that makes him or her enjoy fall's foliage more? What are some things nature has that technology doesn't?

Art, Literature and the World

Literature

451. William Cullen Bryant, a poet and journalist, said that autumn was "the year's last, loveliest smile." What does Bryant mean when he says it's the last smile of the year? Would you agree that it's the loveliest smile as well? Why or why not?

452. Poet Percy Bysshe Shelley wrote about leaves falling from trees as if they were ghosts being driven away. How would the season be different if falling leaves actually were ghosts? How would raking be different? How would the ghostly leaves act and why?

453. Fall is the "mellow time" according to Irish poet William Allingham. Would you agree with him? What are some of the ways in which the fall is mellow for you? What are some ways in which it is the opposite? Which is the most mellow season for you and why?

454. In George Cooper's poem "October's Party," the leaves, sunshine, weather, and wind all come to play in a giant celebration for the season. Imagine that all these things could walk and talk and dance. What would their fall party be like and why? How would it change if humans were invited and why?

455. The fall season may be cause for us to be sad and sympathetic for the

trees that are losing all their leaves, according to poet Robert Browning. Create a conversation between a tree losing its leaves and yourself. Would the tree be sad? Why or why not? How would you describe the fall, winter, and spring to a tree that didn't understand?

456. Sir Walter Scott, a Scottish poet, said that if a tree doesn't blossom in the spring, you certainly won't see fruit on it in the fall. Why do some people expect to get the "fruits" of success without putting in the necessary work first? What are some aspects of your life that require hard work first and why are they worth it?

457. There are people who would rather summer never end and transition into fall, according to author Hal Borland. These same people unsuccessfully hope the world will do exactly what they want. Why is it important to realize that some things are out of our control? How does it feel to accept that something is going to happen?

458. British humorist Thomas Hood said that many of the wonderful aspects of nature, including butterflies, fruits, flowers, and birds, were completely absent in November. Do you miss those aspects of nature as much as Hood? Why or why not? What are some of the more positive aspects of November?

459. Chuang Tzu, a 4th century Chinese philosopher, said that opinions are like autumn, gradually changing and passing away. How have your opinions changed in the last few years? How do you think they will change in the future? Do you think Chuang Tzu is right? Why or why not?

460. According to Italian philosopher Umberto Eco, not only do opinions change, but the way we look changes like autumn as well. How do you think your looks will change as you get older? Which do you think is more important, what you have on the inside or what you have on the outside and why?

Entertainment

461. Television producer and writer Mitchell Burgess said on the show *Northern Exposure* that fall was a time for reflecting on the past. What are some of the ways that you look back at things that have happened in the past year? Do you think reflection is important? Why or why not?

462. The Kinks song Autumn Almanac lists all of the aspects of fall, from the colder weather to the musty yellow leaves, as things you have to deal with. If you made a list of everything that happened during the fall, how would it make you feel? Do the parts of the season you like make up for the parts you don't like? Why or why not?

463. In the movie *Planes, Trains, and Automobiles*, the main characters take any means necessary to get home for Thanksgiving. If you were stranded far away from home on turkey day, how would you try to get there? Would you take anyone with you for companionship? Why or why not?

464. The narrator in the song Autumn by the Edgar Winter Group states that the birds don't have much to say in the fall because they know what's coming. How do you think birds and other animals feel about the post-summer season and why? Do they actually know what's coming? Why or why not?

465. The movie *October Sky* shows the character Homer Hickam become inspired when he sees the first satellite launched into space during the fall. Have you ever seen something in the sky that inspired you? If so, what was it and why did it make you feel that way? If not, what would be something that you might see in the sky that could motivate you and why?

466. The song October by U2 states that even though Kingdoms rise and fall, October will continue to go on. How do you think the world will change in the next few hundred years while October stays the same? While it change for the better? Why or why not?

467. Many inspirational sports movies like *Remember the Titans*, *Hoosiers*, and *Rudy* are set during the fall. If you could write your own touching fall sports tale, what sport would it be about, what would happen to the main character and why would people enjoy it?

468. The narrator in Justin Hayward's song Forever Autumn says that he wishes he could migrate south with the birds after his love left him. What would the fall be like if you were able to fly along with the birds and go south for the winter? How would living with the birds be different than living at home and why?

469. In multiple films, poems, and songs, autumn is referred to as a time when adults are getting older and winding down their lives. How do you think your parents will spend their later years of retirement and why? How will you spend your retirement years and why?

470. In Van Morrison's When the Leaves Come Falling Down, the narrator talks to a girl who thinks about "the wisdom of the leaves and their grace." Would you consider leaves wise and full of grace? Why or why not? How would you describe leaves and why?

History

471. Elias Howe obtained the first patent for a sewing machine in September, 1846. How would the world be different if everybody still stitched clothing by hand? What are some of the ways that sewing machines large and small are used today?

472. In the fall of 1900, Orville and Wilbur Wright began experimenting with their first airplane in the beach town of Kitty Hawk, North Carolina. Imagine that you were in the tiny gliding plane on the first test drive. Would you be scared? Why or why not? What do you think people living in the year 1900 might think of their invention and why?

473. Tools similar to the rake were used in China in 1100 B.C.E. to harvest

hay and grain. What do you think it would have been like to deal with outdoor chores over 3,000 years ago? What would your excuses be to get out of the work and why?

474. In the early 1970s, the rake was replaced in some garages by the world's first power leaf blower. Consumers actually modified an insect spray device by removing the tank and the company began to realize they had leaf-blowing gold on their hands. What are some other tools that you think should be replaced by technology? What would the replacements do better and why?

475. Germany became the first country to use daylight savings time in 1916, allowing us to spring forward and fall back. What are some ways in which you could use the extra hour given to us during the fall other than sleeping? Why would this be a good use of your extra time?

476. In the fall of 2008, a team of Oxford University scientists revived an old refrigerator design patented by Albert Einstein in November, 1930. Even though it was created more than 70 years earlier, the design was thought to be more environmentally friendly. What are some ideas from the past that you think could or should be brought back to the present and why?

477. Sir Isaac Newton helped to develop the beginnings of modern mathematics in the fall of 1666 with what would later be called calculus. Why do you think creating an advanced system of math would be important? What are some things that might not have been invented if it wasn't for advanced calculus?

478. The first jack-o'-lanterns could be found in Ireland but they were made of turnips, potatoes, and beets as opposed to pumpkins. What do you think would be the strangest fruit or vegetable to use for a jack-o'-lantern? What kind of face would you carve into it and why?

479. It took over 200 years for Thanksgiving to become a national holiday, after Abraham Lincoln declared it officially in 1863. What other famous events from U.S. history should be made into national holidays? When would they be celebrated and what would some of the celebratory traditions be?

480. The first official fall football game was played in 1869 between the College of New Jersey (now Princeton University) and the Rutgers University. How different do you think the game might have been from the sport we watch today? How might a star from today do if he or she played back in 1869 and why?

Around the World

481. Munich, Germany is the host to one of the largest fall festivals in the world, Oktoberfest. Attendees drink from giant mugs or glass boots and eat delicious sausages. Imagine that you have created a festival for a different month (such as Septemberfest). What kind of event would it be, what activities would be available, and what types of food could you get there?

482. November 5 is a public holiday in London to commemorate a failed attempt on the king's life by a man named Guy Fawkes. Guy Fawkes Night is filled with fireworks, costume parties, and burning effigies of Guy Fawkes. Have you ever been notorious for something? If so, what was it for and how did you try to clear your name? If not, what might it feel like for someone to think you were the bad guy or girl?

483. Mexico is known in the fall for its early November celebration of Day of the Dead. Families celebrate the lives of their deceased relatives with candies, parties and dancing. What would it be like if there was a similar holiday celebrated in the United States? Would it feel strange to dance and sing in a cemetery? Why or why not?

484. The White Night is a celebration in Paris, France on the night of October 1 in which all museums, monuments and tourist attractions stay open all night and are accompanied by bright lights and music. If you found yourself in France for the festival, how many different places would you try to see? Which might you enjoy the most and why?

485. Jodhpur, India hosts the Rajasthan International Folk Festival every October, bringing together more than 100 musicians from around the world. Do you think it's important to experience music from different cultures? Why or why not? What country's music would you want to see the most at a festival like RIFF and why?

486. Not all international events happen in a physical place. Filminute, an international one-minute film festival, happens online throughout the month of September. As technology continues to improve, do you think that more events will be held online? Why or why not? Would you rather go to an event in person or online and why?

487. The last Sunday of every November is the annual Monkey Buffet Festival in Lopburi, Thailand. The festival is a literal feeding frenzy for the many monkeys who live in the area. What kind of animal do you think your town would feed instead of monkeys during an animal food festival and why? What would be the most difficult part about putting it together and why?

488. Approximately 300,000 people and 20,000 camels gather every November for the Pushkar Camel Fair in Pushkar, India. Describe what it might look like to ride a camel through the festival. Imagine how the fair would be decorated and write out the possible details.

489. Sydney, Australia is the site for the Crave Sydney International Food Festival every October. Top international chefs and visitors come to the city to cook and taste the best of Australian cuisine. Imagine that you were hosting a party with a menu created by chefs from around the world. What different cultures would you and your friends feast on and why?

490. In October, the city of Bacolod, Philippines hosts the Masskara

Festival in which over 400,000 people wear brightly colored masks. Imagine that you could disguise yourself with a mask that made everybody think you were someone else. What person would you pretend to be and why? What would you do while everyone thought you weren't you? Why?

A Mixed Bag #5

491. While picking apples, your family has decided to compete to see who can get the most in an hour. How do you ensure that your basket is fullest by the end of the hour? Who in your family do you think would win and why?

492. What do you think is the secret ingredient to a perfect fall apple pie? If you successfully used this ingredient, would you tell people the secret? Why or why not? What are some recipes you know that use secret ingredients?

493. In a major sight to see, all of the jack-o'-lanterns on your block have grown orange legs and started marching down the street. What happens next? Do you ever find a cause for this phenomenon? Why or why not?

494. Do you think you will enjoy pumpkins as much when you're an adult as you do now and why? How much do your parents like pumpkins and why?

495. You have been commissioned to create a fall festival for your school or neighborhood. Who do you bring on to help you and why? What role does everybody play in the planning process and why?

496. What would be the most important aspects of this fall festival and why? What would be the activities for the adults and what would the kids do for fun? What kinds of food would be there and why?

497. Because of Halloween, fall is a time for extremely scary movies. Do you have a favorite kind of scary movie? Why or why not? Are there certain kinds of scary movies you won't watch? Why?

498. Fall is also the time for starting a brand new year of school. What are some of the feelings you have at the start of a school year and why? Do you think other people feel those feelings too? Why or why not?

499. Create a made-up story using the following words: foliage, pumpkin patch, frightening, and backpack.

500. If you were to carve a different jack-o'-lantern to represent different members of your family, what would they look like and why? Make sure to go into great detail for each one and to explain what each member would think of them.

WINTER

Nature, Activities and Events

Weather and Nature

501. Imagine that you and your family are stuck inside because of a massive snowstorm! What activities will you do while you're inside for a couple of days? How will you feel being unable to exit your front door and why?

502. It is thought that no two snowflakes are exactly the same. What do you think it means to be unique? Would you call yourself unique? Why or why not?

503. When it's cold and icy out, there are a lot of things in your town that may have to slow down or stop. What are some examples of parts of your area that wouldn't be able to work like usual? How might those stoppages affect you and why?

504. In your efforts to find a great hill for sledding, you and your friends have gotten momentarily lost in the snowy forest. How would you find your way back home? What would your first course of action be and why?

505. Some animals grow a heavy coat of fur during the coldest months of the year. Imagine that humans were fur-growers as well. How would your life change with a thick coat of hair? How might winter be different for you? Why?

506. Since most of us don't grow a fur coat every winter, we need to wear the proper winter equipment. Describe your winter clothing from the top of your head to your toes. What is your favorite winter clothing item and why?

507. During the winter, it can get so cold outside that without a coat you can get sick. What are some of the things that can happen if you don't protect yourself from the temperature? What are extra precautions you can take to be warm during the winter?

508. Imagine that the snow from a storm was so strong it knocked over the trees in your neighborhood into the power lines and shut off the electricity. What would your family do with no power in the middle of the coldest season? How long would it take the power to come back and why?

509. If you could be any winter animal, which would you be and why? How would your life be different in the winter than in the summer? What would you miss about being a human and why?

510. What are the best parts of snow and why? What are the aspects of snow that you dislike and why? Do your parents share the same opinion as you? Why or why not?

Activities

511. Imagine that you and your friends created a snowman or snowwomen who has come to life before your eyes! What would this snow person have to

say? What would you all do together and why?

512. While shoveling snow from the driveway can be fun, it's also a lot of hard work. Describe an afternoon of shoveling with your family. Who does the most work? Who complains the most? How do you all celebrate after your accomplishment and why?

513. Imagine that you are in the midst of a massive snowball fight involving everyone in your entire neighborhood. Describe what it would look like to see so many snowballs flying through the air. How would it feel to be hit with one?

514. Your family has purchased the fastest sled on the market and you are extremely excited to take it down the steepest hill in the neighborhood. How do you feel when you're about to sled down the hill and why?

515. One shape that's easy to make in the snow is a snow angel. What are some other drawings you might make in the snow with your body? Do you think it would be easy for your friends and family to tell what you're drawing? Why or why not?

516. There are some days that it is just too cold to go outside. On a day like that, what would your favorite indoor activity be and why? Would you rather do outdoor winter activities or indoor winter activities and why?

517. You and your friends have embarked on a scavenger hunt to find various winter objects outside. What are some things that you might look for? Which would be the most difficult to find and why?

518. Imagine that you and your family have decided to take a nature hike around your neighborhood. How would the plants, animals, and houses look different in the winter than they do in the summer? Would you rather go on a winter hike or a summer hike and why?

519. After a long day of hanging outside in the snow, it's important to come back home and warm up. How do you warm up after a full day of winter? Why is it necessary to get warm and toasty after all that chilly weather?

520. What is your favorite snow activity? Why do you enjoy it so much? Who would you pick to do that activity with you and why?

Sports

521. After a confusing series of events, you are standing at the top of the most difficult black diamond ski mountain in the world. As you begin skiing, you wonder how you got yourself into this mess. How did you end up at the top of this challenging mountain and how will you successfully make it to the bottom?

522. There are people who refuse to forego their jogging habit during the winter and go out running despite the cold and the ice. What might some of the difficulties of running be in the snow and why?

523. In parts of the world like Canada, ice hockey is more popular than

basketball and football because there is always a fresh patch of ice available to play on. How would your life be different if ice hockey were the major sport in your town? What hockey skills might you focus on improving and why?

524. Even though figure skating is a beautiful and difficult sport, it is usually thought of as a sport for girls instead of boys. Why do you think that is? How tough would figure skating be for most people and why?

525. In an attempt to win the grand prize money for your town, you have entered into a snowmobile-racing contest with other people your age. Describe your race as you speed around the course attempting to win. Why might the race be difficult? Who would win and why?

526. Imagine that you have just sped down the hill and gone flying into the air on a ski jump. What would it feel like to be high up in the air with the snowy landscape below? What kinds of tricks might you want to try during your jump? How hard would it be to land and why?

527. Snowboards look similar to skateboard and surfboards. How are the three boards used differently in various sports and climates? Which of the three would you most like to learn to use and why?

528. You are one of the dogs preparing to pull a sled as part of a race. Create a conversation between yourself and these other dogs as you get ready for this difficult challenge. What might you and the other dogs have to talk about and why?

529. Imagine that you and your family have challenged yourselves to go climbing up the side of an icy mountain. How would you keep from falling? Who do you think would have the most trouble with the task and why?

530. What is your favorite winter sport to participate in and why? What is your favorite winter sport to watch? Why?

Events

531. You have been entered into a snowman contest along with over 100 other participants. Your creation will be judged on its face, its expression, and its roundness. What kind of snowman do you make to try to win the event and why? What might your prize be for winning?

532. One major event that occurs during the winter is the lighting of trees for the holiday season. Imagine the biggest and most colorful tree you can think of. Describe what the tree looks like and why it might make such an impact on you. Would it win any awards? Why or why not?

533. You and your family have wandered into an ice maze, which is kind of like a hedge maze mixed with an igloo. How will you find your way out of this confusing tunnel of snow and ice? Would you face any challenges in trying to get your family to go in the same direction? Why or why not?

534. Ice sculpting has become such a major activity that there are ice

sculpting contests and even ice sculpted castles in various parts of the world. If you were an ice sculpting master, what would you use your skills to create and why?

535. While some love everything about the winter, others want to get a taste of spring in the midst of the cold with indoor nature and flower shows. Do you ever feel like you need a break from winter? Why or why not? If you needed a break, how would you take it and why?

536. Many winter events focus on the upcoming holidays like Christmas and Hanukkah. Do you think it's important to get your holiday gifts ahead of time? Why or why not? What gifts are you hoping to receive this holiday season?

537. Other winter events center on chocolate and candy. What kinds of desserts are you more likely to eat during the winter? How would those differ from summer desserts and why?

538. Since being outside can give you a chill during winter, there are a lot of events you can go to that are inside, like a concert or play. What is your favorite kind of indoor performance and why? How much hard work do you think the performers have to do to get ready for the audience?

539. Imagine that you and your family were trying to go to an event but all of the major roads were closed down with snow. How might you try to recreate an exciting event in your own home? What would you do, who would participate, and how fun would it be?

540. The Polar Bear Club is a group of thrill-seekers who jump into freezing-cold water to raise money for charity during the winter. Do you know anybody who would be interested in such a freezing swim? If so, who would it be and why? If not, imagine that you had to do it as part of a dare. How might it feel and why?

A Mixed Bag #1

541. Ski resorts often create some fake snow to improve the safety and appearance of their mountains. Imagine that you could create real snow anywhere you wanted just by thinking about it. How would you use your powers? What would other people think about your chilly abilities and why?

542. If you could be any wintry animal in the world, which one would you be and why? What would your typical day be like? What parts of being a human might you miss and why?

543. You have moved into a house completely made out of ice! Describe how you'd deal with the following challenges: getting up and down the stairs, playing with a pet, taking a bath, and keeping warm.

544. Imagine what winter might be like before there were snowplows, shovels, and salt for the roads. How difficult would it be to get places? How

would your family get food? What would you do for fun?

545. What would life be like if you and your family hibernated like bears during the winter? Would you get bored sleeping for most of the day and staying bundled up for months at a time? Why or why not?

546. Winter is the perfect time to do things inside and around the house. What are your three favorite indoor activities? Do your parents think these activities are a good use of your time? Why or why not?

547. Imagine that it was so cold out that your parents have bundled you up with clothes to the point that you could barely move. How would you walk and talk in this restricted state? What would other people think of your puffiness and why?

548. What do you think it would be like to be the following animals during the winter and why: horse, gorilla, deer, and Chihuahua?

549. Create a made-up story using the following words: ice, nose, mittens, and excitement.

550. What is your favorite winter moment of all time? Why does it stick out for you so much in your memory? What do you think would have to happen to top it and why?

Science and Snacks

Food

551. There's nothing like a hot bowl of soup on a chilly winter's day. What other hot foods tend to warm you up during the coldest seasons? Which is your favorite toasty food and why?

552. Imagine that you and your family are hiking up the side of a snowy mountain. While taking a small break, you take out a bag of trail mix. What kinds of nuts, seeds, and other items might you find in your energizing snack pack? Why might you need energy to keep going up the side of the mountain?

553. You have invited all of your friends over for a winter chili cook-off! What ingredients do you use in your chili? What does your chili taste like? Do you win? Why or why not?

554. The perfect hot chocolate has much more than a simple mix combined with hot water. What other treats would you put into your ideal hot chocolate to heat you up after a long day of playing? Would your parents approve of your recipe? Why or why not?

555. While you might wish that a warm plate of cookies or brownies was waiting for you every day after school, it certainly isn't the healthiest choice. What might happen if you ate brownies all winter long? What are some more nutritious choices and why?

556. Your parents have put you in charge of making a delicious, hot winter meal of macaroni and cheese. Will you come up with your own recipe or use the stuff from the box? How long would it take you and why? Will your parents appreciate your efforts? Why or why not?

557. On a trip out of town, your parents have given you permission to make a waffle in the hotel's waffle maker and to put any toppings on it you want. What toppings do you choose and what does your breakfast taste like?

558. Imagine that you've been shrunk down to the size of a raisin! As you swim around your bowl of morning oatmeal trying to get your parents' attention, you decide to go exploring. Where do you go next and how do you get yourself out of this tiny predicament?

559. Some of the best winter meals come from the slow cooker, which can take hours and hours to use effectively. Imagine that you had to make a meal that took more than five hours. What would you do with your time while you waited for it to cook and why?

560. What is your family's go-to meal during the winter? Why do you think your parents cook it so often during the chilliest months? Would you change this frequent meal to another one if you had a choice? Why or why not?

Animals

561. Imagine that you and your family members were polar bears instead of humans. How would your usual routine change? What would you do for food? Would it be tough living in the snow? Why or why not?

562. Some birds fly south during the winter to find warmer areas of the country. What are some reasons they might migrate? Would your family ever consider taking the few months of winter on a warm island? Why or why not?

563. Birds aren't the only organisms that migrate, as beetles and worms burrow deep into the soil to spend the winter in a warmer environment. What is the warmest part of your house? Do you ever cuddle up in it to keep toasty on a cold day? Why or why not?

564. A frog can hibernate during the winter at the bottom of a pond underneath the frozen water. How would your winter be different if you spent three straight months hiding and sleeping? What are some of the things you might miss and why?

565. During hibernation, bears can sleep as long as six months, during which time they don't eat, sleep, or use the bathroom. What would happen if you fell asleep for six straight months? What kind of things might you miss? How would you catch up and why?

566. Squirrels and other animals stockpile nuts during the warmer months so they have food all winter long. Imagine that your family couldn't go shopping during the snowy season and had to buy everything beforehand.

What foods might you have to skip? What foods would you eat all the time and why?

567. Some insects actually change into different forms during the winter to stay warmer and safer. Imagine that you could change into something else during the coldest months of the year. What would you change into and why? What would your parents think of your transformation?

568. You and your friends are using tracks in the snow to figure out what animals have been running around in your backyard. What do the tracks look like and what animals do you assume have been there? How do you find more evidence to prove your hypothesis? Are you correct? Why or why not?

569. Animals may grow warmer fur or have their fur change colors to match snow during the winter. What are some ways that you adapt to the cold temperatures?

570. If you could be any winter animal, which one would you choose and why? What would be some of your new challenges as this icy season animal? What would you enjoy the most as this animal and why?

Plants

571. In the months leading up to winter, plants develop cold hardiness, which allows them to handle the upcoming colder months. Imagine that your skin and body changed during the winter. How would it change and how would it improve your resistance to the cold?

572. Another winter preparation step for plants includes not growing during the winter. Why might plants be more vulnerable to the cold if they kept growing? What might happen if you gave plants a lot of food right before the winter and why?

573. You and your family have taken up winter vegetable farming, harvesting veggies like broccoli, Brussels sprouts, cabbage, kale, and onions. What might be difficult about harvesting these crops in the winter? Would you enjoy the dishes made from these vegetables? Why or why not?

574. Annuals are plants that live only one year, die off at the end of summer and then leave their seeds to survive the harsh winter months. What would it be like to live an entire lifetime in only one year? What are some things annuals miss out on by only living one year?

575. Some seeds can live over one hundred years buried deep in cold soil before they germinate. How tough do you think pregnancy would have been on your mom if you were in her womb for twice or three times as long and why?

576. Trees that live near the Arctic change during the winter to produce sap that is extremely sweet and sugary. Not only does this keep the tree from freezing, but humans can harvest the sap to use on pancakes. What would it be like to take the syrupy sap directly from one of these trees and why?

577. Like squirrels, some plants start storing food in the form of bulbs and tubers during the fall to prep for the winter. Create a conversation between two plants during the winter, bored of eating the same old stored food all winter long. What do they talk about and why?

578. Some trees have adapted to hold off budding new leaves until they can tell that winter is over. Do you think that winter feels different from spring? How is it different? How might a tree be able to feel the difference between the two seasons?

579. Conifers, including pine trees, make perfect Christmas trees because their leaves don't fall off before winter. Why might their leaves be able to survive the harsh temperatures of winter? How would you compare the appearance of a pine tree to a tree without any leaves?

580. What are some ways in which winter plants and winter animals could work together for survival? Why would it be a good idea for them to help each other out?

Science

581. Because of the way the Earth tilts in relation to the sun, winter on one side of the world would actually be the same months as summer on the other side. How would your life be different if January was one of the hottest months and why?

582. If you lived at the North Pole, you would experience 24 hours straight of darkness on the first day of winter. What would you do differently if you were sun-free for an entire day? Would you miss the daylight? Why or why not?

583. Winter storms are the result of both warm and cold air masses, which is why some of the weather is rain while some of it is snow. What are some of the challenges of a rainy and snowy winter storm? What might your parents tell you to do during such a storm?

584. In March 1993, a winter superstorm led to snow, wind, rain and low temperatures in 26 different states. Imagine what would happen if a winter storm were to affect the entire country? How might your life be affected and why?

585. While it seems really cold at 0 degrees Fahrenheit, there have been winter temperatures recorded that are 100 degrees below Fahrenheit! What clothing might you need to wear to protect yourself from such cold temperatures? Why wouldn't you want to live in an area that gets that cold?

586. Snowflakes grow into beautiful six-sided crystals because of the way that water looks at a microscopic level. Imagine that you could shrink down to the size of a snowflake; what would it look like from this perspective and why?

587. The body shivers when it's cold because the brain sends signals to the muscles to move around quickly to generate heat. What are some other ways

that you generate heat when you're cold? Why does moving around keep you warmer than simply sitting in the snow?

588. Wearing a hat is important during the winter because approximately 50 percent of body heat can be lost through the head. Imagine you could make your own winter hat from scratch. What would the hat look like and how would it keep you warm during the coldest months?

589. Frostbite and hypothermia can occur if you stay out in the cold too long without proper clothing on. What are some other winter dangers that can happen if you don't take safety precautions? How can you best stay safe during winter and why?

590. Driving a car during the winter is extremely dangerous because there is much less friction between the car's tires and the road. What might it be like to drive a car on an icy road? What things would you need to do to be as safe as possible and why?

A Mixed Bag #2

591. You've been chosen to lead a winter expedition in the North Pole on the first day of winter. With harsh elements and no sunlight, how will you succeed in your mission? What tools would you need, who would you take to help you, and why?

592. Create a conversation between two sleigh dogs on your expedition. Do they enjoy working for you? Why or why not? If they had the choice, would they be running at the North Pole or somewhere else and why?

593. There's nothing like burrowing under a large pile of blankets on a chilly night. Write a story about your family all snuggling into one bed covered in blankets. Describe the blankets in great detail as well as how they make you feel.

594. In the not-too-distant past, families had to make their own clothing and blankets to protect against the bitter cold of winter. What kinds of clothes would your family make and why? How would you contribute to the process and why?

595. Imagine what it would have been like to get around in your neighborhood during a snowstorm before cars were invented. What would you do if you needed to get to school or work? What other conveniences might you not have that far in the past?

596. Will it be easier to deal with snow and ice 100 or more years in the future? What inventions might your generation and future generations create to take the bite out of the season? Which would be your favorite to use and why?

597. What are some activities that you love to do during the winter? Which is your favorite and where would you do it if you had the choice? Why might it be tougher to do that activity in a different season?

598. What are the extra chores you might have to take on during the winter? Which is the easiest one and why? Which is the most difficult and why? Do you have fun doing any winter chores? Why or why not?

599. Some parents get very overprotective during the winter. Would your parents fit that description? Why or why not? How do you think your parents acted during a snowstorm when they were your age and why?

600. You have been selected to design a completely winter-proof house. What would it look like, what materials would you use, and who would live in it? Would the house be tough to live in during the summer? Why or why not?

People, Facts and Fun

Holidays

601. Would you shop any differently for someone who celebrates Hanukkah or Kwanzaa than you would for someone who celebrates Christmas? Why or why not? Would you still give gifts to someone who doesn't celebrate any of the three? Why or why not?

602. Do you think the countdown to the end of the year for New Year's Eve is important? Why or why not? Will celebrating the end of the year get more or less important as you get older and why?

603. What are some of the ways that a typical family celebrates Christmas? What are some ways that this family could spice things up by changing around some of their traditions? Do you think it's necessary to be normal? Why or why not?

604. Explain the differences between how an adult celebrates Valentine's Day and how a kid celebrates the holiday. Do you think the holiday is more important for people who are young or people who are older and why?

605. Imagine that Martin Luther King, Jr. was coming to speak at your school. How would the people in your town react? How would getting to hear the great orator in person make you feel? What might you learn from his speech and why?

606. Christmas, Hanukkah, and Kwanzaa have been cancelled for the year. What would you miss about these holidays the most and why? Do you think you would appreciate them more after they were gone? Why or why not?

607. While Christmas is at its core a religious holiday, many people who don't practice Christianity will still celebrate parts of the holiday. Why do you think that is? Do you think people who don't follow the more pious aspects of the occasion still deserve to get the fun parts? Why or why not?

608. Imagine that because of a health condition, you have to eat much more healthfully during Christmas, New Year's Eve, and Valentine's Day. How will

this change the way you eat and drink at these holiday celebrations? Which foods would you miss eating the most and why?

609. You have been asked to visit a friend's house during his Kwanzaa celebration. What questions would you ask to understand the holiday better? How would you feel being part of another culture's holiday and why?

610. What are some of the ways in which we have benefitted from the work of Martin Luther King, Jr. and other important activists? How might the world be different today if none of them had stood up for what they believed in? How would your life be personally different and why?

People

611. You are a bell ringer for the Salvation Army at the local grocery store, trying to raise money for those in need during the holiday season. What are some of the challenges you might face in fundraising? Do you think you'd do a good job? Why or why not?

612. The city is covered in snow and as one of the only snow plow operators in the area, it is your time to shine. What would it be like to operate this big piece of machinery to clear the roads? Would it be scary? Why or why not?

613. Professional ice sculptors have the ability to create beautiful things out of a block of ice. What kind of training do you think you'd need to become one of the best in the business? How would you feel, knowing that your beautiful creations would eventually melt, and why?

614. How would your life be different if you were a professional figure skater for the Olympic team? How hard would you need to work to stay at the top of your game? Would you be nervous having the entire world watch your performance? Why or why not?

615. As a gardener in a cold climate, the winter is not your time to shine. What are some ways that you could keep up your profession during the winter? What would you miss the most about the other seasons and why?

616. You begin to shiver on the sidelines of the conference championship in your biggest National Football League game yet. How will you handle the winter weather of Lambeau Field in Green Bay, Wisconsin? What position do you play and what will you do to ensure your team's victory?

617. It's Christmas Eve and you're working as a cashier in the busiest toy store in the city. How do you handle the unruly customers, the lengthy lines, and the desire to be at home? Is it worth getting paid extra? Why or why not?

618. You make the most delicious chocolates in the world and you can't wait to sell them on Valentine's Day. What is your favorite kind of chocolate to make and why?

619. A birth defect has caused you to have a handicap that affects your legs.

What are some of the challenges you face during the winter? How would you overcome these obstacles? How would you feel not getting to participate in all of the physical winter activities and why?

620. You are a pilot for a commercial airline. What is it like flying through the difficult winter conditions? Do you ever feel nervous about the snow and ice? Why or why not?

Facts

621. A thin, transparent layer of ice that forms on roads and bridges, called black ice, can cause even the most able-footed person to slip. Who in your family would be the most likely to slip on this practically invisible ice and why? What is your typical reaction when you slip on ice and why?

622. On January 28, 1887, a 15-inch-wide, 8-inch-thick snowflake fell in Fort Keogh, Montana, the biggest ever to fall to the ground. What would you do if you found such a huge snowflake plummeting to the earth? How would you make sure it lasted long enough that you could get a world record?

623. In the winter of 1779-1780, 20 feet of ice piled up along the Delmarva Coast. Imagine that you were a fisherman living in the area at the time. What would you do to keep your business afloat during such an icy incident? How would you keep your boat safe while it was nearly covered with ice?

624. Some people get moody and have low energy during the winter due to a condition called Seasonal Affective Disorder. What would you do if you were depressed all winter long to try to keep yourself happy? Who might you ask to cheer you up and why?

625. Chionophobia is the fear of snow and being trapped in the snow. Have you ever been afraid of snow? If so, what was the situation and why were you scared? If not, what might be a situation that would cause you to be terrified of getting trapped in the snow and why?

626. Multiple Canadian schools took on a challenge to create a record of 15,851 snow angels in 2004. What would it have been like to interact with so many people to create snow art? Would you have enjoyed it or thought it was weird? Why?

627. Even during the smallest of snow storms, billions of snowflakes will fall to the ground. Imagine what it would be like to slowly plummet to the ground surrounded by your snowflake friends. What would the view be like? Which would you enjoy more, floating through the air or lying on the ground in a clump and why?

628. Many ancient cultures celebrated the winter solstice by constructing monuments or holding wild celebrations. How would you have chosen to celebrate the solstice thousands of years ago? What would your family today think about your celebration idea and why?

629. Antarctica, a continent that is winter-like all year long, is the home to many whales, seals, and penguins but very few people aside from scientists. What would it be like to conduct experiments on climate, glaciology, and Antarctic animals while living in such a cold and dark place? What location in the world might you rather want to use as a base for your experiments and why?

630. Skiers have used many different terms for snow, including dust on crust, pow pow, and mashed potatoes. What are some slang terms you might use for the powdery substance? Which term would be most likely to catch on with your friends and why?

Festivals

631. Mardi Gras is a wild celebration in the French Quarter of New Orleans, Louisiana, that involves parades, jazz, and beaded necklace-wearing that precedes the season of Lent. If you knew you were about to give up something for a long time, would you indulge in it the day before? Why or why not?

632. Cedarburg, Wisconsin, plays host to the Cedarburg Winter Festival every February, which includes a game that combines golf and tennis on a snow-packed course. If you could combine two different sports, which would they be and why? How would you play the game and would your friends enjoy it? Why or why not?

633. The Fire and Ice Winter Fest in Lava Hot Springs, Idaho, will test the cold hardiness of any man or women as it holds both a costumed tubing water race called the Polar Bear Float and a bikini and Speedo jog called the Running of the Bulls. Would you rather participate in such events or sit back and watch the crazy folks and why? If you did participate, what do you think you'd get out of it and why?

634. The Steamboat Springs Winter Carnival in Steamboat Springs, Colorado, features an event in which people sit on shovels and are pulled down the wintry street by horses. What might the horses think about such a silly event and why? Would you get a thrill out of participating in such an event? Why or why not?

635. Minnesota's St. Paul Winter Carnival includes an event in which inventors create robotic snowplows that race against each other. If you were a robotics genius, what types of things would you try to get a robot to do and why? What would other people think of your invention and why?

636. The Blanket Toss is an event at the Anchorage Fur and Rendezvous Festival based on a native Alaskan tradition in which a person is tossed high into the air from a blanket to look for whales in the ocean. What might it feel like to be thrown over 10 feet into the air? Would you be scared, at peace, or somewhere in between and why?

637. The Thunderbird American Indian Dancers Annual Dance Concert & Pow Wow gives people in New York City the chance to hear traditional stories and music by natives of the continent. Do you think it's important to learn about other cultures? Why or why not?

638. Utah is full of hot air in the wintertime as a result of the Bluff International Balloon Festival. Hundreds of hot air balloons from all over the world float into the sky during the January event. If you had a hot air balloon, where would you fly it to and why? Describe what your typical balloon view would be like.

639. The Winter Wings Festival in Klamath Falls, Oregon, allows participants to watch thousands of bald eagles land during their migration between Oregon and California. Would you enjoy the hobby of bird watching? Why or why not? Who in your family might enjoy the hobby more than you and why?

640. As the winter gets slushy, competitors in Bellaire, Michigan, race down the Schuss Mountain wearing crazy costumes as part of the Slush Cup Weekend. What kind of costume would you choose to ski down a mountain in and why? Would you win a costume contest in that getup? Why or why not?

A Mixed Bag #3

641. How did ice get so cold in the first place? Create a mythical origin story to explain how and why the ice became the way it is.

642. Create a story using the following words: frozen, Zamboni, hot chocolate and championship.

643. Write a conversation between two marshmallows floating at the top of a frothy hot cocoa. What do they have to talk about and why?

644. Write a poem about a lonely snowflake wafting through the air without any of its snowflake friends. How did it get separated from the rest of the snow and why?

645. Imagine that you were building your own snow amusement park. Write four or five slogans or catch phrases that you could use to advertise your park online or on TV.

646. Describe the perfect winter video game or app. What would you do during the game, what would you do to win, what would be the most fun part about it, and why?

647. Create a song about a snow plow operator battling the elements during the biggest blizzard in a decade. Will he succeed in his or her attempt to clear the streets? Why or why not?

648. Describe the plot of a made-up movie during the winter. What kinds of characters are in the film? What genre is it? Would the movie be a big hit? Why or why not?

649. Write a letter, e-mail, or long text message to a relative to explain what you've done so far this winter. Explain everything in great detail. Would you leave anything out? Why or why not?

650. A strange occurrence has left you holding a message from your future self, a decade into the future during the winter. How is your winter in the future different from your current winter and why? How will you and your family have changed?

The Five Senses

Sights

651. How does it feel to wake up and see the world covered by a blanket of white snow? What is the first thing you would do and why? Would your feeling change if you found out you still had school? Why or why not?

652. Imagine that the snow was piled so high that it completely blocked your window. Would your feeling be any different? How would your parents feel if they saw the snow piled that high and why?

653. What would you do if you saw a person slip on an icy patch of sidewalk and why? Would you do the same thing if it was a family member or a complete stranger and why?

654. How would your reaction change if you saw a car spin out and crash into a snow embankment? Do you think that most people would do the same thing as you? Why or why not?

655. What is the most memorable thing you've ever seen during the winter and why? What would have made the event less memorable? How would your memory change if you heard about it in a story instead of experiencing it first hand?

656. How do you think the event would have been different if you were blind and could only use your other sense to observe it? Would it have been as memorable? Why or why not?

657. How do you feel when you see a large pile of Christmas, Hanukkah, or Kwanzaa gifts and why? Do you ever do anything special to try to figure out what the gifts are? Why or why not?

658. How would the sight of all those gifts affect you differently if you were very poor? Why is it important to remember people who are less fortunate than you during the holiday season?

659. Which of the following events would you rather see and why: the Winter Olympics, the Super Bowl, New Year's Eve in Times Square, New York, the lighting of the biggest Christmas tree in the world?

660. How would attending that event make you feel and why? Who would

you want to accompany you and why? How would the event be different if you saw it alone?

Sounds

661. What does the sound of a massive, diesel-powered snow plow going by your house make you think of and why? Would it make your parents think of something different than you? Why or why not?

662. How might you feel about the sound if you were the one driving the plow? Would you take pride in your job? What would you enjoy the most about your job plowing the streets and why?

663. As you look out into the vast snowy landscape, you hear a gust of wind blowing the snow from one hill to another. If the winter wind could talk, what would it say and why? How would you respond to the howls of wind and why?

664. Create a poem or a song that describes how the winter wind sounds differently than the wind of other seasons. Include how the different seasonal winds make you feel and why for a personal touch.

665. When the roads are covered in snow, the sound that can stand out the most is the sound of silence. How does the quiet and white road make you feel in comparison to its usual noise level and why? Is there anything you are more or less likely to do because of the quiet and why?

666. If you lived in a frequently snow-covered area, would you get sick of the quiet? Why or why not? What sounds would you most want to hear if you hadn't heard any in a while and why?

667. It seems like the entire neighborhood is gathered at the top of the steepest hill in town. Describe the sounds of all the kids as they sled, tube, and dive down the snow-packed hill. Which of the sounds do you like, which do you dislike, and why?

668. How do you think the way sounds of kids sledding and enjoying themselves make you feel will change as you get older? Will you be jealous, annoyed or something completely different and why? Would this feeling change if it was your own kids playing? Why or why not?

669. What are some of the sounds you hear around your home in the winter that you wouldn't normally hear in other seasons? How do those sounds make you feel and what sounds might you use to respond to them?

670. You hear a large group of Christmas carolers down the street heading toward your house. How will you and your family react and why? Would you react differently if you were a different religion or lived in a different neighborhood?

Smells

671. The holiday season can be a bit overwhelming with the delicious smells of Christmas, Hanukkah, and other festivities. Which is your favorite of the

holiday smells and why? What would that smell make you think of it you happened to get a whiff of it while walking down the street and why?

672. Gathering with family during the season can bring a great many odors together, from your aunt's perfume to the baby powder of a newborn cousin. What is your most memorable family smell from your most recent winter holiday gathering and why? Is it memorable in a good way or a bad way and why?

673. After a long weekend day of playing in the snow, what scent would you most want to smell upon returning home and why? What does that smell usually mean is about to happen and why?

674. After that day of play, what would you least want to smell and why? How would that smell make you feel and why? What would you do to avoid that smell and its consequences and why?

675. How would you describe the smell of a winter's day? If you were to take in that smell during a different season, what would it make you think of and how would it make you feel? Do you like the smell? Why or why not?

676. How does winter smell differently compared to the other three seasons? How would it make you feel if you noticed the aroma of winter more than a month early and why? Would the possibility of extra winter excite you or disappoint you and why?

677. As you take off your many winter layers, you notice that even you smell a little different during the season. How has your scent changed in the wintertime and is it for better or worse? Would that aroma alteration cause you to make any changes? Why or why not?

678. If you could choose a smell of winter to bottle up and wear as a cologne or perfume, what would it be and why? How would people react differently to you if you smelled like that aspect of winter and why?

679. How do you think the smell of winter has changed in the last century with more cars on the road, ice-melting chemical salt, and snow blowers? How would your neighborhood smell differently way back then and why? In what other ways would your area be different?

680. How might the smells of winter change in the next 100 years and why? Would new technology produce better-smelling chemicals or worse-smelling ones? Will the winter become more or less environmentally friendly and why?

Taste & Touch

681. How would you describe the taste of snow? Why do you think people enjoy sticking their tongues out during a snowfall? If you could give any flavor to snow, what would it be and why?

682. You are holding a huge snowball in your glove-protected hand. How does the texture of the snow feel through the glove? How would it feel

differently if you weren't wearing gloves and why?

683. There are many different varieties of hot chocolate you could drink during the winter, including from a packet, with or without marshmallows, and topped with whipped cream. What do you think is the best-tasting hot chocolate in the world and why? Describe the taste of this treat in great detail.

684. Imagine that your hands are absolutely freezing until someone gives you a cup of hot cocoa to hold onto. How does the toasty cup feel on your hands? Why is it important to keep your hands warm during the winter?

685. What is your favorite taste of the holiday season and why? Would this be a taste you'd want to have all year long? Why or why not? Would it still be as special if you had it every day? Why or why not?

686. Imagine that you have just picked up your first gift to open during the holidays. How do the wrapping paper and tape feel against your hands? How do you feel when you finally get to tear into it and find out what it is and why?

687. Your family has decided to sit by the fireplace and have your favorite winter dish. Describe all of the courses of the meal and how they taste. Does the meal change at all because you're eating it by the toasty fire? Why or why not?

688. How does the warmth from the fireplace feel on your skin? How does it change the way you feel on a cold winter's night? How might a winter indoor fireplace feel different than an outdoor campfire during the spring or fall?

689. Is there anything your parents drink or eat during the winter that you dislike? If so, what is it and what does it taste like to you? If not, come up with a made-up food or drink and describe why you dislike it.

690. There are many winter items like matches, kerosene and lighters that kids aren't allowed to touch. Why do you think it's a good idea for children not to touch these fire-starting objects and substances? What are some other winter items you aren't allowed to touch in your house and why can't you touch them?

A Mixed Bag #4

691. How do you think the country would be different if we were in the middle of a wintry ice age? What are some ways that you and your family would do things differently and why?

692. If there were an ice age afoot, how would the country's economy change? How would it effect agriculture, shipping, and air travel? How do you think we as a nation would adapt to the weather and why?

693. What are some ways in which a town can come together to fight back against a winter storm? Who are some of the people who need to communicate during a storm and why? What is the end result of these people working together?

694. What would happen if these people failed to work together during

some harsh winter weather? What problems might your town face and why? What would you do to try to improve the situation and why?

695. You have been tasked with thawing out and starting a car that has been completely frozen over with a thick sheet of ice. What would you do to get it loose? Who would you ask to help and why? Would you be successful? Why or why not?

696. How might your tactics change if you were a rescue worker and there was a very cold person trapped inside the icy vehicle? Describe how you'd get the person out of the car and what you'd do afterward to make sure he or she was alright.

697. If you lived in a consistently cold and icy climate, do you think you'd be drawn to an ice-related sport like ice hockey or figure skating? Why or why not? Would there be any sports you play now that you wouldn't be able to participate in? Why or why not?

698. Imagine that you are the goaltender in an outdoor ice hockey game with over 100,000 people watching you. How do you feel and why? What are some ways that you handle the pressure? Do you think you would win? Why or why not?

699. Who is someone you know who strongly dislikes the winter? What does he or she have such an issue with the season? If you wanted to convince this person that winter was awesome, what would you do and why?

700. People living in certain climates have never experienced a cold, snowy, and icy winter. How might they be unprepared for the season if they took a vacation to a wintry place and why? How would you personally help this person and why?

Art, Literature and the World

Literature

701. A proverbial saying related to winter states that a rich man gets his ice in the summer and a poor man gets his in the winter. What do you think that means and why? What other things might a poor person not be entitled to that a rich person could have all year long?

702. In the 16th century, winter was used in literature as a symbol of old age. In what ways does winter make you think about aging? If you were writing a poem about winter, would you use winter to symbolize something different? Why or why not?

703. Shakespeare's play *A Winter's Tale* sets half of the play in the winter during the reign of the cold-hearted King Leontes. Do you think that some people act differently during the winter? Why or why not? Might these same people literally become warm emotionally during the warmer months? Why or

why not?

704. The phrase lion in winter, used as the title of James Goldman's play *The Lion in Winter*, refers to a strong and important person who has become old and less important because of age and hardship. Do you think that you will get better with age? Why or why not? Why might it be tough to be strong when you reach a certain age?

705. *Richard III*, another Shakespearian play, refers to a time of unhappiness as "the winter of our discontent." Have you ever had a winter of discontent? If so, what made your winter so unhappy and why? If not, imagine and write about what you would have to do to get yourself out of a winter funk.

706. George Herbert, a poet famous for his pattern poems, once wrote that "every mile is two in winter." What might he mean literally and figuratively by that? What are some of the aspects of winter that seem long and why?

707. British poet Edith Sitwell wrote that winter is a time for home. Why do you think home is especially important during the winter? Imagine that you had to spend winter far away from home. How would it be different?

708. Anne Bradstreet, who wrote the first book by a woman that was published in the United States, wrote that "if we had no winter, the spring would not be so pleasant." Would you agree with that statement? Do we need to have the unhappy side of something in order to fully experience its happier side? Why or why not?

709. Writer and fiction editor for *The New Yorker* Katherine S. White, once wrote that one of the three gardens of winter was "the garden of the mind's eye." What might she mean by that? What are some of the things you might use your imagination for during the winter and why?

710. In Shakespeare's *Love's Labour's Lost*, the character Biron says that there are certain things that make sense in each season. He wouldn't want a rose in winter just like he wouldn't want snow in the spring. Do you ever hope for warm weather in the winter? Why or why not? Do you think having an appropriately snowy winter is important? Why or why not?

Entertainment

711. In Joni Mitchell's song Urge for Going, she makes it seem like everyone and everything wants to leave when winter closes in. Would you say that's accurate? Why or why not? Have you ever felt like leaving your town for greener pastures during the winter? Why or why not?

712. In the movie *An Affair to Remember*, the character Terry McKay said, "Winter must be cold for those with no warm memories." What does it mean to have a warm memory? Would you agree that people without that kind of memories would act colder? Why or why not?

713. The narrator in the song California Dreamin' by the Mamas and the

Papas states that he'd be "safe and warm" if he was on the west coast during the coldest months. Would you rather live in a place that was warm all year round, even if you'd miss out on playing in the snow? Why or why not?

714. In the famous horror movie *The Shining*, the main character goes crazy when he's cooped up in a hotel in the middle of nowhere during the winter. Do you ever get restless when you're not able to go outside in the winter? Why or why not?

715. The song Early Winter by Gwen Stefani refers to an impending breakup as an "early winter." Do you think of an early winter as an upsetting thing? Why or why not? Why do you think songs and poems often use winter to refer to something negative?

716. The movie *Groundhog Day* shows a grumpy newscaster having to re-live the same winter day over and over again until he gets it right. What would you do if you had to live the same 24 hours over many times in a row during the winter? How would you pass the time and why?

717. The television show *St. Elsewhere*, a medical drama from the 1980s, ended its series by revealing that the entire universe of the show was the daydream of an autistic child staring into a snow globe. What would you do if you found out that part or all of your life was nothing but a dream? How would you live life differently and why?

718. The movie *The Day After Tomorrow* shows part of the world descending into an ice age with the people having to survive the new landscape. How would your life change if your town became year-long arctic wasteland? Would you consider moving? Why or why not?

719. In the *Seinfeld* episode The Strike, we are introduced to a winter holiday called Festivus that includes a metal pole and an airing of the grievances. If you could create a winter holiday, what would it be called, what activities would it involve, and would your family enjoy it? Why or why not?

720. In the bleak winter movie *A Simple Plan*, a group of friends and family members find $4 million worth of cash in the middle of nowhere. What would you do if you found that much money that didn't belong to you and why? Would the situation be different if you found the cash with some friends? Why or why not?

History

721. One of the most famous American winter events is when George Washington crossed the Delaware River with his troops in 1776. What might it have been like to be under Washington's campaign during such a treacherous journey? Would you have considered deserting the Army like many troops did at that time? Why or why not?

722. In the winter of 1967, the Midwest saw one of the biggest blizzards of all time, which dumped more than two feet of snow with winds exceeding 50

miles per hour just days after tornadoes and temperatures in the 60s. How would you stay safe during such a wintry storm? How would you prepare for it in the first place?

723. During one of the strangest moments in Winter Olympics history, the ex-husband of figure skater Tonya Harding set up a sneak attack on Harding's rival, Nancy Kerrigan, to try to knock her out of the competition. Imagine that someone tried to sabotage you during a test, game, or sport. How would you respond and why?

724. The winter of 2011-2012 was one of the warmest winters in history. What sorts of things would you do on a warm winter day that would be different from a regular spring or summer day? Would you appreciate the warmer day more in the winter or during another season and why?

725. When the armies of Napoleon Bonaparte and the French invaded Russia in 1812, they were unable to handle the Russian winter and eventually had to abandon the campaign. Imagine that you planned a major event, only to be stopped by tough winter weather. How would you feel? What might you do instead and why?

726. In an effort to avoid the freezing winter in 1778, British navigator Captain James Cook took his crew south during an expedition and became the first Brit to find the Hawaiian Islands. Imagine that you were looking for an object and came upon something much, much better. What might it be? How would it be better and why?

727. During the winter of 1873, 15-year-old Chester Greenwood invented the earmuffs to protect his ears. If you could come up with any winter invention, what would it be and why? Do you think it could be as successful as Greenwood's? Why or why not?

728. Norwegians Carl Howelsen and Angell Schmidt introduced ski jumping to the Western United States in 1911 in Hot Sulphur Springs, Colorado, spurring an extremely popular ski industry in the mountainous state. What would it be like if you could introduce something in a foreign land? How would people treat you? How would you feel and why?

729. In the 1988 Olympics, the Caribbean island of Jamaica sent its first representatives to the Winter Olympics as part of the bobsled team event. What do you think winter would be like for you if you'd only previously experienced a tropical beach environment? What challenges might you face and why?

730. *Snow White and the Seven Dwarfs* was released into theaters in December 1937, and it was the first full-length animated movie. Imagine that you were the first person to do or create something. What might that thing be and why? How would you feel after doing it?

Around the World

731. In China, the Dongzhi Festival is a Winter Solstice festival in which people eat brightly colored rice balls and worship their ancestors. Which of your ancestors might you want to honor during such a holiday and why? Do you think it's important to remember your family's past? Why or why not?

732. Sadeh, a Persian festival, celebrates fire and its ability to keep away frost, cold, and dark. How important might fire have been in your life if you lived over 100 years ago and why? Does fire still play a role in your life today? Why or why not?

733. On January 13, some Ukrainian, Belarusian, and Russian cultures celebrate Malanka, a night of playing pranks, acting out plays, and dressing men in women's clothing. What would such a festival be like in your neighborhood? Would you enjoy it? Why or why not?

734. Canada's Quebec City holds a Winter Carnival every February that is filled with music, art, parades and dogsled races. What would your life be like if you needed a dogsled to get to school every day? How would you take care of the dogs? What would your sled look like?

735. One of the largest international snow sculpture contests can be found on Japan's Hokkaido island in the city of Sapporo every February. If you wanted to win the Yuki Matsuri contest, what would you build and why? Who would you recruit to help you?

736. Up Helly Aa is a winter festival held in the Shetland Islands, United Kingdom, in which residents dress up like Vikings and burn down a replica ancient ship. Imagine you could bring a real Viking from the past to see this festival. What might he think about it and why?

737. During the winter, Siberia's 400-mile Lake Baikal completely freezes over, giving way to major festivals taking part on top of the ice. If all of the water in the world froze over for a week and you could travel anywhere by car or bus, where would you go and why? What would it be like traveling on the slick, icy, former lakes, rivers, and oceans?

738. In France, the story of Santa Claus is slightly different: children put out their shoes to collect presents and add beet greens to feed the donkey that Santa rides. Would you want to try out how different cultures celebrate Christmas and other holidays? Why or why not?

739. The winter holiday Bodhi Day, a part of Buddhist cultures, is less about food and celebrations and more about sitting and thinking. What kind of ideas could you come up with if you sat and thought more often? Do you think it's important to have some quiet time to yourself? Why or why not?

740. Diwali is a major holiday in India that includes a festival of lights, food, and other celebrations. The winter holiday is celebrated in different ways depending on what region of India you live in. What tweaks would you add to

American winter holidays if you had a choice? Would these changes catch on? Why or why not?

A Mixed Bag #5

741. If you could create a piece of artwork to represent winter, what would it look like and why? What kind of materials would you use? What would people think if it got put into a museum and why?

742. You've discovered a time capsule full of old pictures and newspaper clippings of the people who lived in your house during the winter of 50 years ago. Describe all of the contents of the time capsule. What might you learn about winter in your town from this discovery and why?

743. You've been entered into a winter obstacle race with an exciting first place prize. What are some of the winter-themed obstacles? Which might you have the most trouble with and why? What's the prize and do you win it?

744. Which of the following competitions would your family be most likely to win and why: winter holiday house decorating, skiing relay race, ice hockey match, or partner figure skating contest?

745. Create a made-up story using the following words: icicles, snow blower, frostbitten, and triumph.

746. What are some ways in which your winter diet is different from your summer diet? In which season do you eat more healthfully and why?

747. How would your winter change if you had a heated hot tub in your backyard? How would you use this toasty device to melt away your winter blues? Which of your friends might come over to use it and why?

748. Imagine that you and a friend or family member have started a business shoveling neighbors' driveways for a fee. How much money would you charge, how long would each driveway take, and how difficult would it be? How would you feel to be working in the freezing cold and why?

749. While digging up snow in your backyard, you find a cave person completely frozen in ice! What happens next? Are you happy about the end result of your find? Why or why not?

750. Describe your ideal snow day. Where would you be, what would you be doing and who would you be with? How would such a day make you feel and why?

SPRING

Nature, Activities and Events

Weather and Nature

751. On a sunny spring day, you and your family have decided to create a garden. What are some of the fruits, vegetables, and other plants you would include? What might be the toughest part of gardening and why?

752. It's been said that April showers bring May flowers. If you had a choice between a rainy April day and a day in May walking among the flowers, which would you choose and why?

753. Imagine that you had the biggest back yard in town and could use this grass-covered area to do whatever you wanted. What activities would you take part in using this wide open space? Would people come over to your house more often? Why or why not?

754. Create a conversation between two blooming flowers in the springtime. What would their thoughts be on the season and why?

755. A baby duck has lost its way and thinks that you're its mother! How will your day change now that you have a little duckling following you around everywhere you go? What will you do to make sure your duck has a healthy and happy life and why?

756. As you and your friends lie in the grass, you look up to the clouds and see what shapes you can see. What people, places, and things do you see mimicked in the white, puffy clouds? Do your friends see the same objects that you do? Why or why not?

757. Imagine that you could understand what birds meant when they sang throughout the treetops. What do you think they most often talk about and why? What would it sound like if you tried to sing back and why?

758. Spring is a time of birth and renewal for plants and animals as they go through their life cycles. What does plant and animal renewal mean to you and why? Do you think humans take part in this renewal process as well? Why or why not?

759. It is the first day of spring that's warm enough for you to go outside without a coat on. What will you do with this coatless freedom and why?

760. You and your friends are off to collect items and pictures for a spring scrapbook. What kinds of things would you find or photograph for the scrapbook that represent spring? What might you think when you look back on the scrapbook 10 years in the future and why?

Activities

761. Even though you're ready to go outside and play, your parents say that

it's time for spring cleaning. What are some of the chores you might have to do during a big cleaning session? Which is the chore you least enjoy doing and why?

762. The rain is in full force, and after getting your parents' permission, you put all of your rain gear on and start splashing in as many puddles as possible. Describe what it's like to splash in a giant puddle. What do you enjoy about it the most and why?

763. Imagine that you have caught a talking bug in a jar. What does the insect have to say to you about nature and the life of a bug? Would you let him free if he asked you to? Why or why not?

764. The breeziness of spring makes it perfect weather to fly a kite. What kind of kite would you fly if you had a choice and why? Where would be the best place for kite flying? Who would you ask to come with you and why?

765. Your family has planned a picnic and you get to choose the menu. What foods would you want to bring and why? How would those food choices change if you had to cook the food yourself?

766. After noticing the birds in your neighborhood don't seem to have a place to stay, you've recruited a group of friends to create a collection of bird houses. What kind of houses would you make for the birds? How would these houses be different than your family's house and why?

767. It's so rainy outside that your parents want you to play inside today. What are some of the things you do in your house when it's pouring outside and why? In what ways can you use your imagination to come up with other playful indoor ideas?

768. While blowing bubbles outside with your friends, you've all become trapped in giant bubbles and you've started to float away. Where will you travel in these huge floating bubbles and why? What will your family think when you tell them about your adventure?

769. Springtime is a great time for art. If you could create any kind of artwork during a warm spring day, what would it be and why? What materials would you need to gather for your project? What would the finished piece of art look like?

770. You have been tasked with making up a brand-new game to play with your friends at the park. What will you call the game, what are the rules, and how do your friends enjoy playing it?

Sports

771. What is your favorite position to play in a baseball game? What would it be like if you could play that position for a professional league? How good do you think you'd have to be to make the pros and why?

772. Track and field is particularly popular during the spring. There are

many different events including the long jump, the pole vault and the 50-meter dash. Which event do you think you'd be the best in? Which would you have trouble with and why?

773. Some spring sports like lacrosse have been played for more than 1,000 years. How do you think playing sports would be different that far in the past? Would people in the past have a tough time playing in the modern world? Why or why not?

774. Imagine that you have been given tickets to see the top tennis players in the world play in the nearest city. Would you know any of the top-ranked players' names? What would you enjoy the most about the event and why?

775. Just in time for spring soccer, you have somehow gained super speed and strength. How would you use these newfound abilities on the soccer field? Would it be tough to keep your super powers secret? Why or why not?

776. You have been entered into a major canoe race that's three months away. How do you think you'd train for such an event? What would be the toughest part of rowing a canoe for 10 minutes straight and why?

777. Imagine that you were a professional golfer who was about to putt for a chance to win a major tournament. If you miss, you would lose and let down millions of fans. What kind of pressure do you think you'd be under? What would you have to do to make sure you sink the shot?

778. As part of a local promotion, your favorite baseball player is coming over for dinner during his spring training preparation. Who is the player, what do you feed him, and what kind of things do you talk about? Do you get any signed merchandise out of the deal, and if so, what do you get signed?

779. There are many different games that you can play during the spring that let you run around and enjoy the mild weather. What is your favorite game to play and why? If you could play it anywhere, where would it be and why?

780. After buying a baseball bat you were told had magical powers, you've been able to hit the ball nearly 20 times farther than usual. How would your life change with these new hitting abilities? Would you let anyone else use the bat? Why or why not?

Events

781. There are many spring festivals that allow you to look at the blooming trees, flowers and other plants. Where in the world do you think the best place to attend such a festival would be and why? Who would you take with you and how would you document the festival?

782. You have been invited to a spring food festival, celebrating farm-fresh fruits, cheeses, and meats. Why do you think food tastes better when it's straight from the farm? Would you ever consider living on a farm? Why or why not?

783. Spring is a time for big dances like prom for high school students. Imagine that your town or school had a dance that you were invited to. What would you wear and what kind of dances would you learn in preparation? Would you have a good time? Why or why not?

784. It's spring break and you have been given the choice to go anywhere you want! Where would you choose and how would you get there? What would you do during this exciting vacation?

785. Imagine that you have written a play to be a part of an international theater festival going on during the spring. What would the play be about? Who would star in it? Why was it selected to this prestigious theater celebration?

786. National Park Week in April allows nature lovers to visit their favorite national parks like Yosemite for free. What do you think you'd see at a national park that you wouldn't see walking around your local woods? What might be an image at the park that you remember for a lifetime and why?

787. You've been challenged to a pie-eating contest at a local spring festival. How will you train for this speedy eating event? What kind of pie would you choose to eat? Would you win? Why or why not?

788. During spring flower shows and other plant events, gardeners spend many hours caring for their creations in hopes of winning a prize. Do you think you'd be able to put in the time necessary to grow a prize-winning plant? Why or why not?

789. As part of daylight saving time, we spring forward one hour and set all of our clocks accordingly. Imagine that you accidentally went an entire year into the future. How would your life change? What would you have missed in the previous year? Would you be able to get back? Why or why not?

790. Imagine that you could create your own spring festival. What aspects of spring would you celebrate, where would you hold the event and what would it be called? Would people enjoy this new celebration? Why or why not?

A Mixed Bag #1

791. Spring is a time for many new plants to grow. What are some ways that you've grown in the past year? How do you think you'll change and improve in the next few years? Why?

792. Winter can be too cold and summer can be too hot, but spring is usually the most comfortable temperature of all the seasons. What are some places and things that make you feel comfortable? Why do they make you feel that way?

793. Imagine life as a bird during the spring making your home in a giant, leafy tree. What kind of things would you normally do throughout the day? What food would you eat? What would you do for fun and why?

794. What is the most beautiful thing you've ever seen during the spring?

What made this picturesque scene stick out in your mind? How did it make you feel to look at it and why?

795. Describe what it would be like to have a spring break at the following locations and why: lake house in the woods, cherry blossom festival in the country, giant parade in a major city, and the tropical rainforest?

796. Create a made-up story using the following words: grass, hike, growing, and party.

797. Imagine what spring might have been like during the age of the dinosaurs. How might plants and animals have been different? How do you think the spring might have changed since that time and why?

798. Describe how a spring thunderstorm might be difficult for the following professions and why: airplane pilot, lumberjack, gardener, and professional pole vaulter?

799. How do the smells of spring differ from the other three seasons? How do spring smells make you feel? What makes spring smell the way it does?

800. Imagine that you are a tiny seedling trying to sprout during the spring season. What would be the obstacles to you successfully sprouting? What kind of plant would you become if you became fully grown and why?

Science and Snacks

Food

801. Many spring meals consist of fresh fruits and vegetables. If you had a choice, would you rather eat something fresh or a food from a box or can and why? Is your favorite spring meal fresh or processed?

802. In honor of spring, you're hosting a party at your house with all of your friends. What foods will you put on the menu to both celebrate spring and impress your guests? What are some foods you absolutely wouldn't choose and why?

803. One of the simplest spring desserts is combining fresh strawberries with whipped cream. Would you say that you have simple tastes or that you like things with a lot of different flavors and why? Would you make a good food taster? Why or why not?

804. You have been chosen to create the best and most nutritious salad the world has ever seen. Where will you go looking for these tasty spring ingredients? Would you eat the salad yourself? Why or why not?

805. The spring is the season for the incredible, edible egg! The happiest and healthiest chickens tend to make the tastiest eggs. How hard do you think it would be to treat a chicken right? What steps might you have to take to make

sure your chicken was the best she could be and why?

806. Once you have the eggs from your healthy, happy chicken, what will you do with them? What are five different ways you could use eggs in meals? Which would be your favorite and why?

807. Your family has been entered into a fruit pie baking contest and all of you have to help. Which baking task would each of you take and why? What kind of spring pie might you make and why?

808. Some of the best spring seasonings include mint, oregano, rosemary, cilantro, and dill. What are your favorite herbs that you or your parents use to spice up your food? Why is it important to use herbs instead of just salt and ketchup?

809. Fresh cheese straight from the dairy farmer is a wonderful spring treat. What are your favorite uses for cheese? Would you rather have it on a sandwich, a pizza, or on something else? How do you think fresh cheese would be different from processed cheese and why?

810. Imagine that you were a rabbit running about the neighborhood during the spring. What kind of vegetables and plants would you look for to eat? Do you think you would be healthier as a human if you ate like that rabbit sometimes? Why or why not?

Animals

811. Many animals have their babies in the spring because of longer days and plentiful amounts of food. Imagine that you found a lost baby animal and had to take care of it until you found its family. What would the animal be? What would you have to do to take care of it? Would you enjoy being an animal parent? Why or why not?

812. Birds sing beautiful songs to find their mates for the spring. Do you think this is a good process for picking someone to spend your life with? Why or why not? If you were a bird, would you add any other things to look for? Why or why not?

813. How do you think humans would be different if they had to lay eggs during the spring and sit on them until they hatched? Would your parents take turns on the eggs? Would you have to sit on the egg of a baby brother or sister? Why or why not?

814. The many migrating birds that left during the fall and winter return home during the spring to find mates and have babies. Why do you think the birds don't just stay in one warm place? What might be some reasons they feel the need to travel hundreds or thousands of miles twice a year?

815. Hibernating animals like hedgehogs, bats, bears, and squirrels begin to wake up from their long slumber during the spring. How do you feel after you've taken a long nap? What might you need to do to completely wake up?

How would that compare to a hibernating bear and why?

816. Even though they're cute, rabbits can wreak havoc on your backyard garden as they look for food to eat. Imagine that you have been hired as the guard of your parents' garden. What would you do to scare the rabbits away from your parents' carrots? Would you be successful? Why or why not?

817. Monarch butterflies take part in a wild yearlong journey including a move from Mexico to Texas and Florida at the beginning of the summer to lay eggs on the milkweed plant, the only plant monarch caterpillars can eat. What would happen to these butterflies if the milkweed went extinct and why?

818. After the trip to Mexico and the southwestern United States, these butterflies can go as far north as Canada during the spring and summer before the cycle continues. What would it be like to be one of these globetrotting butterflies? Would you enjoy all the traveling? Why or why not?

819. Upon noticing hundreds of salamanders trying to cross a nearby street to get to a spring mating pond, you and your friends decide to build a tunnel to keep the amphibians safe. How do you get this tunnel approved? What do you use to create the tunnel? What is the end result and why?

820. While mating seasons occur during the spring in most areas, animals in tropical climates don't stick to one particular time of year. Why do you think that is? What would you do differently than you do now if you lived on a tropical island and why?

Plants

821. The beautiful blooming flowers of spring include daisies, irises, and lilies. What would it be like if humans could bloom? What would they look like and why?

822. One blooming flower that can be considered a weed is the dandelion. How do you think this green and yellow plant spread itself throughout the whole world? Are there any plants you'd rather were as common as the dandelion? If so, what plants and why?

823. While some people don't like them, dandelions have many helpful properties and have been used in medicine and for coffee substitutes. What is an example of something in your life that has many different uses? What do you use it for and why?

824. Imagine that you have been invited to a festival to watch the blooming of a really ugly spring plant. What would the plant look like? Why would everybody be celebrating it if it was so strange-looking?

825. While some flowers need to be planted months in advance to flower in the spring, many trees need to be tended to for years or decades to reach their full potential. Do you think it would be worth it to care for a plant for more than a year? Why or why not?

826. You are a small insect living on a plant in a huge spring garden. What kind of plant would you want to live on and why? How would your insect life be different from your human life and why?

827. Have you ever planted a seed to watch it grow? If so, did it turn out how you expected? Why or why not? If not, imagine that a seed you planted turned out to be something wildly different than you thought it was. Describe the mystery plant in great detail.

828. Spring is the best season for strawberries to get the freshest and juiciest berries. Create a conversation between two strawberries discussing how they hope to be used by humans. What are some of their options other than simply being eaten?

829. Naval oranges are best picked during the spring. What is the freshest orange juice you've ever had? What would you have to do to get it even more fresh? Would the juice taste different if the fruit came straight from the tree? Why or why not?

830. Imagine that you could plant an entire farm of your favorite spring fruits. Which ones would you choose and why? Would you want to take part in the farming yourself or would you rather just eat the fruit and skip the work and why?

Science

831. Spring and the other three seasons are the result of the Earth spinning while tilted at 23.5 degrees. What would it be like if you couldn't walk around straight because you were slightly tilted all day long? What challenges would you face in everyday tasks and why?

832. The constellations Virgo and Leo are visible at night during the spring but they can't be seen at all during the fall. Why is it that we see different constellations in different seasons? Do you enjoy stargazing? Why or why not?

833. As the spring days get longer, plants start to wake up from their winter slumber by forming buds and growing again. What are some changes that you undergo during the spring? How would those changes be different during an unseasonably chilly and winter-like spring?

834. Create a conversation between two sprouting seeds in the ground. What do these soon-to-be fully grown plants have to discuss? What are some of the challenges of being a seed that they might be worried about and why?

835. Imagine that plants needed something different from sunlight and water to grow. What would these new plant requirements be and why? Would it be easier or harder to grow plants with these different needs and why?

836. As the flowers bloom during the spring, bees move from plant to plant helping the plants to reproduce through the process of pollination. Are you afraid of bees? Why or why not? Since bees are so helpful to flowers, do you

think flowers are scared of bees as well? Why or why not?

837. Even though bees are scary, they are necessary to help the growth of a lot of the food we eat. What do you think would happen if all of the bees got sick and couldn't fly? What might happen to the plants and why?

838. Springtime isn't just about plants growing, as kids tend to grow slightly faster in the spring compared with other seasons. Imagine that you had a big growth spurt all season long. How tall would you grow and what kind of changes would you need to make? What would your parents think about your spurt and why?

839. Extra rain mixed with melting snow can cause floods during the spring. What would your family do if it started to flood in your neighborhood? How would you make sure that you could stay safe with the large amount of water whooshing by?

840. As flowers and bees spread pollen, humans can start having allergic reactions such as sneezing and coughing. Seasonal allergies affect millions of people. Imagine that you were allergic to something you enjoyed doing or eating. How would you cope? What would you change to try to replace this enjoyable thing and why?

A Mixed Bag #2

841. While your parents are out of town on a second honeymoon, you have been asked to tend to the spring garden. What kinds of tasks might you need to do to keep it healthy? Will you be successful? Why or why not?

842. When spring break comes around, it's important to clear your head for the last leg of school. What is the best way for you to relax and why? Do you usually feel relaxed upon your return? Why or why not?

843. Spring cleaning is upon us and your parents have locked you in your room until it's completely clean. What area would you have to tackle first? How would you feel while you were cleaning? How would you feel when you're all done and why?

844. Will you think about spring cleaning differently when you have your own house in the future? Why or why not? What will be the toughest party of tidying your own pad and why?

845. You have climbed to the top of the tallest tree in the forest, giving yourself the best view in town. How would this view be different in the spring than it would in other seasons and why?

846. How would the spring view from the top of a tree be different than the view of a furry mouse on the ground? Which of you would have a better view and why? How might the mouse feel about its view and why?

847. Describe the perfect spring day running around playing with your friends. What activities would you do and why? Where would you play and with

whom? How would the day make you feel and why?

848. How would you spend your ideal spring day if nobody was around? Do you think your activities would be the same as other people who are alone during the spring? Why or why not? Would you rather have the alone day or the day with friends and why?

849. What is some music that reminds you of the spring? How is that music different from the music of the other seasons? Which season has your favorite music and why?

850. You have been commissioned to write a song about spring. What would some of the lyrics be and why? What other songs might your song sound like and how would your song be used?

People, Facts and Fun

Holidays

851. While gifts and cards are important, making your mom feel special on Mother's Day is by far the best thing you can do. What are some non-gift ways that you can make your mom feel great during the holiday? Would it be hard to do any of them all year long? Why or why not?

852. If plants and animals had a Mother's Day celebration, how might they celebrate the holiday and why? Which living thing other than humans would have the best festivities and why?

853. April Fool's Day is a time for people to play tricks on others. What are some ways in which nature can pull a prank on you? Do you think nature ever enjoys its occasional sneakiness? Why or why not?

854. The term sophomore, which is used for 10th graders or second-year college students, literally means "wise fool." What does it mean to be a wise fool? Would a holiday for sophomores be any different than April Fool's Day? Why or why not?

855. Imagine that Earth itself celebrated Earth Day. How would the planet decorate itself? What meals would it prepare for the plants and animals? Would it take the day off from any responsibilities? Why or why not?

856. If there was a group of people who most needed to pay attention during the Earth Day celebration, who would it be and why? What would happen if everyone worked hard every day to create a cleaner planet and why?

857. Arbor Day is a spring holiday dedicated to planting trees. If you could pick any area in your town for a new forest, where would it be and why? What would the new forest look like and what would you do in it?

858. What are some ways that you are like a growing tree? Imagine that a tree was planted in your backyard the day you were born. How would the two

of you grow differently? What would it be like to share the same birthday as a tree and why?

859. Memorial Day is a holiday in which we recognize the sacrifices people have made for our country and our freedom. Who are some people you know who have made sacrifices (large or small) for you? How did you show your appreciation for those sacrifices?

860. Many members of the military who fought for our country in various wars did not survive. What is one way that you can honor fallen troops? What are some ways you can honor troops that survived? Why is it important to do both?

People

861. Your friends say that you're the sweetest, but you swear it's the bees that do most of the hard work. As a beekeeper, you do your best to make sure the bees are happy and healthy. What do you like the most about tending to bees? What is your favorite bee product and why?

862. Nearly every day you go hiking and get paid for it. All spring long you serve as a trail tour guide in a beautiful, mountainous, wooded area. What is the toughest part of this recreational job? What are some of the job's benefits and why?

863. You are well known around town for the fine jams, nut butters, and other homemade delicacies you sell at the local farmer's market. It's been said that people are willing to drive 100 miles just for your jam. What is it like to have your products so sought after? What are your secrets for the perfect spring jam?

864. There are many companies whose environmental policies need to be changed to keep the world alive, and you're just the protestor to do it. You create signs and travel in big groups to make sure these companies know how important the planet it. Are your protests ever successful? Why or why not?

865. You love Mother's Day for a couple of reasons. Being a florist, it's both the busiest day of the year and it allows you to show off your hard work. What is the toughest part about working with flowers? How do you feel when you see a happy mother with her bouquet from your store and why?

866. You are a stay-at-home mom or dad. You work harder than anybody realizes and you feel great when Mother's Day or Father's Day rolls around because you are so committed to being a parent. Is working as a full-time parent worth it? Why or why not? What are the main benefits and why?

867. As a minor league baseball player nearing the age of 25, this spring training may be your last shot to make the major leagues. You've worked hard, just like the other prospects, and you hope your game will be at its best. What position do you play, what do you do to train, do you make the team, and why or why not?

868. With the spring chorus concert approaching, you feel like you're working 20 hours a day just to keep your head above water. As the choral director, you are responsible for several hundred kids and their (hopefully) beautiful musical performance. What are some of the songs they'll sing, what are your biggest challenges, and how well do they do?

869. You are the fastest runner in the United States. Your college coach has told you that if you finish in first in the last race of the spring, you could be on your way to the Olympics! Does your final race make you nervous? Why or why not? How did you get to be so speedy?

870. As the head groundskeeper for the largest botanical garden in the nation, you know that millions of people will see the work of you and your team. If a tree's leaves are uneven or if a flower droops, you are responsible. What do you enjoy the most about spring and your job? How do you feel when a family stares in awe at your well cared-for creations and why?

Facts

871. The Pony Express began in the spring of 1860, one of the first innovations in the postal system. After the invention of e-mails and text messages, do you think that sending mail through the postal system is still necessary? Why or why not? What are some things that wouldn't work to send electronically and why?

872. On April Fool's Day in 1946, a huge tsunami stuck many unsuspecting Hawaiians because they thought the warnings were just a joke. What are some things that are too important to joke about? What would you do if you weren't sure someone was telling you the truth or not and why?

873. William Shakespeare, one of the most famous writers of all time, was born in the spring of 1564 and died in the spring of 1616. What do you think it would take for someone to surpass him as the most famous writer of all time? What is it about him and his writing that makes him so well known?

874. April is National Poetry Month. Write a poem about what you think you'll do the rest of this spring and why you'll do it.

875. On April 15th, millions of people will send in their tax returns to the Internal Revenue Service of the U.S. government. Many people put off their doing their taxes until the last possible second. Why do you think so many people procrastinate with their taxes? Do you think you'd get an accountant to do your taxes or do them yourself and why?

876. In May 1888, Nikola Tesla, a brilliant scientist who was ahead of his time, received a patent for alternating electrical current. He later unsuccessfully tried to spread free wireless electricity throughout the world that could have led to the Internet being invented nearly 100 years earlier. Do you think it's important to have people like Tesla in the world who try their hardest to create new and unusual experiments? Why or why not?

877. Over 200 years before the Emancipation Proclamation, the state of Rhode Island passed a law on May 18, 1652 that banned slavery. The law was barely recognized by officials and was not enforced. How do you think history would have changed if slavery was abolished a full 200 years earlier? Would your life be impacted? Why or why not?

878. The first female presidential nominee in the United States was Virginia Woodhull and the nomination occurred in the spring of 1872. She was nominated for the presidency despite the fact that women were not yet allowed to vote. Why is it important for both men and women to be allowed to vote? What could the people in power do if a certain sector of the population was not able to cast a vote?

879. The American Revolutionary War began in the spring of 1775. If you lived back in that time, how do you think you would have contributed to the battle for American Independence? How would your family members have contributed and why?

880. World Health Day is April 7 and while there are sick people in the United States, there are much higher percentages of illness in some developing countries. Would you ever consider going to another country to help to prevent sicknesses like malaria, tuberculosis and other potentially deadly diseases? Why or why not? What are some ways you can keep yourself healthy?

Festivals

881. The Angola Prison Rodeo at the Louisiana State Penitentiary pits prison inmates against bulls, horses, and a series of cowboy activities every April. Imagine that you were stuck in prison for a crime you didn't commit. What would you do to pass the time while you waited for an appeal? Would you be interested in a rodeo? Why or why not?

882. Bay Springs, Mississippi, plays host to the Anvil Shooting World Championship every April in which amateur rocket scientists try to shoot a 100-pound anvil the highest using a rocket. Do you think that rocket science is the most difficult subject to learn? Why or why not? Do you think you could be a rocket scientist? Why or why not?

883. It's not warm and beautiful in every spring festival location. For example, the Big Mountain Furniture Race in Whitefish, Montana, features recliners, toilets and even coffins attached to skis traveling down a snowy mountain. If you could create a racing vehicle out of any piece of furniture, what type of furniture would you use and why? Would you win? Why or why not?

884. Arctic Man is a similarly snowy fall event in which skiers and snowmobilers team up in a race to the bottom of a mountain. If you could participate in any extreme sport, what would it be and why? Do you think it's more important to have a thrill or be safe and why?

885. Paranormal events are those that can't be explained by science, and the ParaQuest Paranormal Conference is held every spring in Lynchburg, Virginia to discuss everything from ghosts to UFOs. Imagine that you saw something you couldn't explain. Who would you tell? Would you try to understand exactly what it was? Why or why not?

886. You'll see a lot more insects in the spring than you will in the winter, and you'll see them flying through the air at Purdue's Bug Bowl in West Lafayette, Indiana. Along with many exhibits and games, willing participants engage in a distance cricket-spitting contest. Do you like playing with bugs or are you scared of them and why? Who in your family would be most likely to participate in the cricket-spitting contest and why?

887. Every spring, robotics experts from around the world bring their robots to San Francisco, California, to battle in the Olympics of Robots. The robots play games, fight, and bowl their way to glory during the competition. What are some of the things that you think robots will be able to do in the future? What tasks might you trust a robot to do for you and why?

888. There is no such Saint as St. Stupid, but that doesn't stop San Francisco residents from putting on the St. Stupid's Day parade on April Fools Day. The parade participants make fun of the city and themselves dressing up in ridiculous costumes and chanting things like, "No more chanting!" What is the stupidest thing you've ever done on purpose? Why did you do it?

889. Every spring on Secretaries Day, residents of Springfield, Missouri, have the chance to throw typewriters from a height of 50 feet in an attempt to hit a bull's eye. How would your life be different if people still used typewriters instead of laptops? What would you miss the most about your keyboard and screen and why?

890. Trivia questions are used in competitions and games to test people on their knowledge of pop culture and the world. The World's Largest Trivia Contest in Stevens Point, Wisconsin, asks teams eight questions an hour for 54 straight hours. Who would you bring with you to help in this wild trivia event and why? How many hours do you think it would take for you to get cranky during the extremely long contest?

A Mixed Bag #3

891. Why did the bee fall in love with the flower and start the process of pollination? Create a mythical origin story about when bees realized that flowers should be a part of their lives.

892. Create a story using the following words: cleaning, honey, forward, and secret.

893. Create a conversation between two bears coming out of hibernation. Did they mean to sleep so long? Why or why not?

894. Write a poem about a caterpillar that is unsure it will ever be able to

become a butterfly. What is the tiny creature so worried about and how did it get so glum?

895. You and your family have started a spring cleaning service for the neighborhood. What are some catch phrases you might put on your car to advertise for the business and why? Will the advertising make you a success? Why or why not?

896. To make some extra money, you've developed a spring-themed game people can play online to celebrate the season. Why do people enjoy the game so much? How hard did you have to work on it and why?

897. Create a song about two neighboring flowers with one trying its hardest to outgrow the other. Is the competitive flower successful? Why or why not?

898. You are the producer of a spring-themed movie and you need to do major re-shoots because audiences hate it. What don't people like about the film? What will you do to try to fix it and why?

899. You have been asked to write a letter to your grandmother or grandfather about your spring. Write the first few sentences of the letter. How would you write this letter differently than you would to a cousin or friend and why?

900. You have received a message from yourself exactly one year in the future. What does your future self have to tell you about this spring and why? Will you do anything differently because of the advice? Why or why not?

The Five Senses

Sights

901. Watching a flower bloom during the spring is not a one-hour event that you could take in during one sitting. There are many tiny steps along the way until the flower has completely bloomed. Would you have the patience to check back with a blooming flower every day to view each step? Why or why not? What are some other ways that nature requires patience?

902. What would you classify as the most exciting process to watch unfold in nature during the spring and why? Why do you think most people would rather look at a computer screen or phone instead of nature? If you had a choice between the two, which would you rather watch and why?

903. There are many beautiful gardens and landscapes throughout the world. If you were to guess which of these places was the most breathtaking, which country or city would you guess and why? Would you rather go there with your family or alone to take in the sight and why?

904. If you lived in this beautiful place and saw the same amazing sights

every single day, do you think it would change your attitude about the importance of nature? Why or why not? What are some ways that your life would be different living in such a picturesque place and why?

905. What is your typical reaction when you see a big plate full of spring vegetables in front of you at the dinner table and why? Does the fact that the vegetables are healthy for you make a difference? Why or why not? How much do you usually finish?

906. Imagine that it's 20 or more years in the future and you have kids and a garden full of fresh spring vegetables. Would you try to force your children to eat the veggies even if they didn't want them? If so, how would you try to make them appreciate the sight of vegetables? If not, what would you feed them instead and why?

907. How do your parents deal with the spring sight of grass that has grown too high around your house? Do they cut the grass themselves? If not, do they hire someone or just let it grow as tall as it can? Do you think that freshly cut grass looks better than an overgrown lawn? Why or why not?

908. How might someone cutting the grass look to you if you were an ant living in the ground? Would it be frightening or cool, and why? What other aspects of spring would look different from the perspective of an ant and how would they make you feel?

909. Your parents have come home with tickets to a spring sporting event. Which kind of spring sport would you be the most excited to see and why? Which type of event would you be least excited to see? How would you best try to enjoy the event you aren't that interested in?

910. Seeing a spring event like a spring training baseball game can be amazing as a kid, but do you think it's just as amazing for the players? If you were a player, what would the sight of a baseball field make you think of, considering that it's your job? Do you think it would be difficult to stay excited? Why or why not?

Sounds

911. The springtime morning can be filled with the sounds of birds chirping away. How does hearing a bunch of birds singing make you feel and why? Would you feel differently if they were singing on a weekend or a vacation and why?

912. If you could understand bird language, what do you think the bird songs would mean? What would you talk to the birds about if you could speak bird as well? How would the birds react to a human singing bird songs and why?

913. Often thought of as an unanswerable spring question, if a tree falls in the woods and nobody is around to hear it, does it make a sound? Why or why not?

914. What are some other questionable sounds that could occur in a forest without anybody knowing about them? What would it be like to live alone in the middle of the woods and be the only person to hear these sounds? Why?

915. Since spring is a season that can cause allergies, a frequent spring sound is the sound of a sneeze. What is your typical first reaction when you hear a sneeze and why? Do you say or do anything when you hear a sneeze? Why or why not?

916. Many different people have very unique sneezes. Which one of your friends has the loudest and most boisterous sneeze? Would you say that sneeze fits with his or her personality? Why or why not? How would you describe your own sneeze?

917. Some sounds during the spring can be frightening, like the buzzing of a bee or a hive of bees. What are the scariest sounds you can think of that you might hear in nature? How would you react if you heard those sounds and why?

918. While we may be afraid of some insects and animals, often they're the ones who are afraid of us. What are some sounds that humans make that might scare a forest creature? What are some machine sounds that could frighten animals? How might you react to the sounds if you were an animal and why?

919. If you were designing a spring video game, what sounds of the season would you include and why? How realistic do you think you'd be able to make the sounds from the game and why? What would the game be about and why?

920. Who that you know would rather hear the sounds of spring from a video game as opposed to experiencing them in nature and why? Why do you think it's important to go out and experience nature during the spring? What are some of the benefits of the fresh air and the activity?

Smells

921. What are some smells that remind you the most of spring? What are some spring memories you might think of while smelling those scents? How would you react the first time you smelled them during the season and why?

922. How do you think the following places would smell differently during the spring and why: New York City, a cow pasture, a lakeside property, and the tropical rainforest?

923. How would you describe the smell of a fresh herb garden? Which of the herbs would stand out the most to you and why? Are there any herbs you wouldn't eat in a million years? Why or why not?

924. How would you react to the smell of a fresh herb garden if you were a bunny? What would you do to try to sneak into the garden to have some lunch? Would you get caught? Why or why not?

925. Of all the flowers you've ever smelled, which one had the most

appealing scent and why? How hard do you think it would be to plant a garden full of those flowers and why? Who would you get to help you and why?

926. How do you think flowers smell to a bee? Describe what might be going through the mind of a bee as she excitedly dances from flower to flower. Is there anything in your life you get as enthusiastic about? Why or why not?

927. As the saying goes, it's important to stop and smell the roses. What do you think this saying means? Would you agree with it? Why or why not?

928. What are some ways that you can "stop and smell the roses" during the spring both literally and figuratively? What usually goes through your mind when you get a chance to relax and take in your surroundings? How often do you think a person should practice this habit and why?

929. What are some smells of spring that completely turn you off and why? What would you do if your parents bought an air freshener that smelled exactly like the worst of those smells? How would it make you feel and why?

930. Based on your enjoyment of spring aromas, would you consider yourself a spring person? Why or why not? Out of all the people you know, who would you say is the springiest person and why? Which season do you connect with the most and why?

Taste & Touch

931. You are biting into a fresh spring salad of raw vegetables. Would you enjoy the taste of the salad without any kind of dressing? Why or why not? Which of the vegetables would stick out flavor-wise the most and why?

932. If you were a gardener, which vegetable do you think you'd enjoy harvesting the most and why? Do you think you would gain a different connection with the food by handling it before it reached your table? Why or why not?

933. Do you think food tastes differently when you eat it outside during a spring picnic? Why or why not? What are some of the tastiest foods you'd bring along on your picnic and why?

934. Some people feel a need to sit on the ground every once in a while and run their hands through the grass to feel connected with the earth. How do you think they feel when they have the opportunity to do so? Do you feel similarly when you're out in nature? Why or why not?

935. Imagine that you were looking forward to biting into a juicy, red apple but it tasted extremely strange. Upon looking at your hand, you realize you were actually eating a tomato. How does the tomato taste differently from how the apple would have tasted? How do you feel about the mistake you made and why?

936. After doing your terrible stand-up comedy routine on stage, the audience has pelted you with dozens of tomatoes. Describe the feeling of the

tomato pulp running down your skin. What is an example of a bad joke the audience didn't like?

937. Describe a spring meal you look forward to every year. Explain how each food tastes to you and why you enjoy it so much. What ingredients do you think are the most important to make it taste exactly how you like it and why?

938. Imagine that you were a cook getting ready to prepare a spring meal. Would you rather handle ingredients that were fresh, frozen, or canned and why? Which do you think would result in the best-tasting meal and why?

939. Think ahead to the future when you're a mother or a father. What would your ideal breakfast in bed be and why? Describe how each ingredient would taste. Would the meal taste differently because your children made it? Why or why not?

940. You and your family members are stitching together a green spring quilt to give as a gift to your relatives. Describe how you might need to use your sense of touch in putting the quilt together. How would the quilt feel if you took a nap underneath it and why?

A Mixed Bag #4

941. How many steps do you think it takes for fresh spring vegetables to make it to your table? What are some ways people might have to work together to send these healthy treats your way? What could happen if they don't communicate or work well together and why?

942. What are some ways in which the different aspects of nature have to work together to grow the vegetables in the first place? What are some things that could happen in nature that would prevent the veggies from growing and why?

943. After a lazy winter, what are some ways you can spring into a more active season? What are a few things that could get in your way of being active and productive and why?

944. Why is it important to be up and about during the spring? What are some benefits of being outside and moving around? Would you rather be active or lie around during the spring and why?

945. Imagine that hundreds of people in your town participated in a huge community garden. What would it be like for so many people to get involved in the planting and why? How would gardening in a big group be different from doing it alone?

946. Several months after the planting stage of this huge garden, what would it look like? Describe the many different plants springing up throughout the plot. How would the people involved feel after working together on such a massive agricultural project and why?

947. Imagine that the showers of April went on for seven consecutive days.

How would the rain affect your community? How would all of the rain change your daily routine? How would the constant precipitation make you feel and why?

948. If it were raining cats and dogs out there, what outfit would you wear to protect yourself? Describe your anti-rain gear from head to toe. What is the most important asset in your outfit and why?

949. Would you consider yourself a flower person? Why or why not? What do you appreciate the most about flowers and why? What are some aspects of flowers you could do without and why?

950. Imagine that you had seasonal allergies during the spring and you started sneezing every time you went outside. How would you spend your season differently from most people? How would you feel if you loved the outdoors but couldn't go outside?

Art, Literature and the World

Literature

951. The poet E.E. Cummings once wrote that "the earth laughs in flowers." Would you agree with Cummings? What are some other ways that the earth might laugh and why? How does the earth laughing differ from the way humans laugh and why?

952. "No spring skips its turn," according to author and journalist Hal Borland. How would the world be different if spring did skip its turn? What would be the parts of spring you'd miss the most and why?

953. Author Geoffrey B. Charlesworth spoke of spring as if it were an orchestra. If spring was an orchestra, what instruments do you think each different type of animal and plant would play and why? What would such spring music sound like and why?

954. April is like a green traffic light that makes the world think "Go" according to poet and essayist Christopher Morley. What are some ways that people "go" during the spring? What are some ways the other seasons make people stop and why?

955. Mark Twain and many other writers have discussed the concept of spring fever as a feeling that makes you want to go out, have fun, and fall in love. What do you think spring fever would feel like and why? In what ways would someone with spring fever act differently and why?

956. Margaret Atwood, an author and environmental activist, once said that at the end of a spring day "you should smell like dirt." Imagine that you have planted a beautiful spring garden with your family and you need to tend to it every day. How would you make time for the garden? Would you have to remove any technological things from your schedule? Why or why not?

957. According to a Chinese proverb, plants recognize spring sooner than humans do. What do you think the first sign of spring is for a plant and why? Aside from the calendar, what is a sign that spring has come for you and why? How do you feel when you realize it's finally spring?

958. Chilean poet and diplomat Pablo Neruda said that "you can cut all the flowers but you cannot keep spring from coming." Why do you think some people remain grumpy even when it's beautiful outside during the spring? If you were feeling unhappy during the spring, what would you do to snap out of it and why?

959. It's important to enjoy how the seasons change from one to another as opposed to simply being in love with spring, according to writer George Santayana. What are some ways you can love the other three seasons as much as you enjoy spring? Would your life be different if you enjoyed the weather and the transitions throughout all the seasons? Why or why not?

960. Wallace Stevens, an American poet, said that spring prepares everyone an annual surprise. Imagine that you did in fact receive a major surprise every spring. What would this year's surprise be and why? What would be some of the surprises the season could hold for you in the future and why?

Entertainment

961. Actor Robin Williams once said that "spring is nature's way of saying, 'Let's party!'" Would you agree with him? Why or why not? What are some ways that nature parties during the spring? Does nature enjoy itself? Why or why not?

962. In the song Suddenly It's Spring, which was famously sung by Frank Sinatra, the narrator feels young and free and starts dancing because it's spring. Has spring ever made you feel the same way? Why or why not? What about spring might cause someone to be that happy and why?

963. *The Secret Garden*, a children's novel that has been made into multiple movie adaptations, shows that having a garden and growing things can be very healing. Who in your life might be happier and healthier if they had a garden to grow and why? What are some aspects of having a garden that you might enjoy and why?

964. The classic 1960 spring break movie *Where the Boys Are* is set in Ft. Lauderdale, Florida. The movie inspired thousands to visit the city the following years, which is an example of life imitating art. What are some ways that movies and television shows have inspired people in real life to do things? Have you ever been motivated to do something because of a movie? Why or why not?

965. The movie *Bambi* shows a springtime in which all the animals fall in love, or as they call it, become twitter-pated. What do you think it means to become twitter-pated? Have you ever been twitter-pated? If so, what did it feel

like, and if not, how do you think you would react and why?

966. *Spring, Summer, Fall, Winter...and Spring* is a movie about a young Buddhist apprentice and how he learns about life cycles from his master. Do you think it's important to be kind to plants and animals? Why or why not?

967. In the movie *It Happens Every Spring*, a scientist accidentally comes up with a chemical that makes baseballs unhittable. He uses the chemical to become a successful pitcher until he runs out. Do you think it would be fair to use a substance to get an advantage in a sport? Why or why not? Would it be considered cheating? Why or why not?

968. In the movie *The Lorax*, based on the Dr. Seuss classic, the spring is completely treeless because the trees were all chopped down to make the Once-ler a fortune. What would you do if a greedy company began cutting down all the trees? How would you try to convince the company's president that trees are important? Would you succeed? Why or why not?

969. A colony of ants is oppressed by some evil grasshoppers in the classic Pixar film, *A Bug's Life*. Why is it important to stand up for yourself and what you believe in? Do you think there are places in the world where people are oppressed by the powerful and ruthless? Why or why not?

970. Set in the beautiful, green countryside, the movie *Pollyanna* follows the life of a girl who learns to be perpetually optimistic despite a difficult life and a crippling injury. Do you think optimism is important? Why or why not? What benefits might an optimist have that a pessimist wouldn't have and why?

History

971. Geoffrey Chaucer's *The Canterbury Tales*, which was set during a spring pilgrimage, was one of the great early contributions to English literature, written in the late 1300s. What are some words you use today that would not have been around over 700 years ago? Do you think you'd have a tough time talking to people who lived back then? Why or why not?

972. The first spring training, a two-month out-of-town training period in which players try out for Major League Baseball teams, started in the spring of 1870 in New Orleans. Imagine that you started the first two months of school touring around the country. Where would you want to go and why? What might you learn during your city-by-city tour?

973. The tradition of spring cleaning may have started with ancient Jewish, Chinese, and Iranian cultures cleaning for various holidays and traditions. What are some other traditions in your household that might have started hundreds or thousands of years ago? How would it be different to do those chores before electricity and why?

974. Spring break is a wild and crazy time for people in high school and college, and the most recent tradition may have stemmed from the city of Fort Lauderdale starting a College Coaches' Swim Forum in 1938. What is the

largest party you've ever been to? Did you enjoy it? Why or why not?

975. In the spring of 1912, the RMS Titanic, a ship carrying thousands of people, ran into an iceberg at full speed and sank. The crew had received warnings of the icy waters but failed to listen. Why do you think it's important to listen when someone gives you advice? Have you ever failed to listen to important advice? What happened and why?

976. The word April means "to open." What are some of the things that open during April? If you could open a new shop or business during the spring, what would it be and why?

977. The first Kentucky Derby was run in the spring of 1875. Create a conversation between two thoroughbred horses getting ready to compete in the biggest event in their lives. Would they be scared? Why or why not?

978. March Madness, a spring college basketball tournament with 68 teams competing for first place, expanded from eight teams in 1939, to 64 in 1985, to 68 in 2011. Imagine that you played for the last place in the tournament. What would you feel like going against the toughest team in the nation? Would you have a chance of winning? Why or why not?

979. Before the Gregorian Calendar was introduced, April 1 used to be part of the new year celebration. When it changed to January 1 in France in the 1580s, some people didn't believe it and were labeled "April fools." Imagine that someone told you something you couldn't believe. What would it be? Why wouldn't you believe it?

980. The first Mother's Day was celebrated in 1914 and quickly became about cards, gifts and other commercial practices. Do you think gifts and other tangible items are necessary on Mother's Day? Why or why not?

Around the World

981. The Cherry Blossom Festival in Japan runs all spring long, depending on when the beautiful flowers blossom throughout the country. Imagine what it would be like to travel through Japan to experience every town's individual festival. How do you think the towns would differ from each other and why? How would seeing the flowers blossom make you feel and why?

982. Thailand is the site of the Songkran Water Festival in which people, statues, and even elephants are enlisted in a three-day-long water fight. If you had a giant water fight in your town, who would you want on your team and why? Would your team be successful? Why or why not?

983. In April in cities around the world, the celebration of Critical Mass is a disruptive occasion in which hundreds of bicyclists ride down the streets of major cities in packs to disrupt traffic. What would it be like to bike in this mass of people? What do you think is the purpose of this celebration and why?

984. The spring is the season for cheese-rolling in Gloucester, United

Kingdom as individuals and teams compete in races to roll wheels of cheese down a hill the fastest. What would you enjoy the most about watching silly people roll cheese down a hill while tumbling themselves? Would you more enjoy watching the people or eating the cheese afterward? Why?

985. Some of the most famous film celebrities will be on hand at the Cannes Film Festival in Cannes, France, during the spring. What would it be like to be an acclaimed and beloved film director? Which movie star would you enjoy working with the most and why?

986. The Feria Del Caballo in Seville, Spain celebrates horses, bullfights and traditional Spanish traditions for two weeks in April and May. If you were in Spain for the festival, would you watch the bullfights? Why or why not? Would you enjoy life as a bullfighter? Why or why not?

987. In the Philippines, the residents love their buffaloes so much that they hold the Pulilan Carabao festival in which they give the mammals a shower, a shave, and a parade. What would your family life be like if you owned and took care of a buffalo? What chores would you have to add to your list?

988. A wild carnival in Copenhagen, Denmark pulls in approximately 200,000 people each spring to show off different kinds of dancing and music from around the world. Imagine that you were an amazing dancer, the best in your town or school. How would you use these dancing abilities and why? What would people think of your skills and why?

989. In Krakow, Poland, the Lajkonik Festival celebrates a major military victory with a re-enactment and an all-night party. What are some of the military victories we celebrate in the United States? Do you think it's important to remember our successes? Why or why not?

990. There are multiple comedy festivals throughout the spring around the world including the Cat Laughs Kilkenny in Ireland and the Melbourne International Comedy Festival in Australia. What do you think it takes to be a funny comedian? Who is the funniest person you know personally? Do you think that person could ever be a professional comedian? Why or why not?

A Mixed Bag #5

991. Create a made-up story using the following words: garden, rabbit, aroma, and picnic.

992. What is the most important aspect of spring to you and why? What is the most important part of spring to your parents and why? Do you think the things you like about spring will change as you get older? Why or why not?

993. Some schools have a Spring Fling dance in which everyone is invited. Would you want to attend? Why or why not? What would you enjoy the most about the dance and what would you enjoy the least? Why?

994. After some hemming and hawing, you decide to attend the Spring

Fling. What will you wear to the dance, what types of dances will you do, and whom will you dance with? Which of your friends would have the best dance moves and why?

995. As part of a challenge, you will participate in 24 outdoor activities in 24 hours (1 hour for each). What are some of the sports you would play? What would be the toughest aspects of the challenge and why?

996. If you couldn't go outside for an entire week during the heart of the spring, what would you miss the most about the outdoors and why? What would you do inside to pass the time and why?

997. Trees can live for a particularly long time, even longer than humans. Describe what a tree might think upon watching a human grow up all the way from infancy to old age.

998. Spring is often referred to as a key part of the life cycle. Do you think it's important that the lives of organisms are cyclical? Why or why not? How do you think it would feel to be an animal or insect with a very short life cycle and why?

999. What are some things that you think about during the spring that you might not think about during other seasons and why? When do you do your most thinking during the day and why is that your best thinking time?

1000. Many creatures we talk about during the spring, like birds, bees, and squirrels, base most of their actions in instinct. Do you think it's important that humans have the ability to go beyond instinct? Why or why not? What are some ways you use reason in your daily life?

ABOUT THE AUTHOR

Bryan Cohen's philosophy is to turn a few ideas into many. This concept was one of the reasons behind his passion of creating thousands of creative writing prompts. His books, including his best-seller *1,000 Creative Writing Prompts: Ideas for Blogs, Scripts, Stories and More*, have sold over 15,000 copies. Build Creative Writing Ideas, a website created by Bryan which contains hundreds of articles of writing advice, helps over 25,000 people a month to get over writers block and come up with new creative projects.

Bryan also writes about comedy, self-help and embarrassing anecdotes from his life. He is also an actor, director and producer who enjoys dabbling in both theatre and film in Chicago, Illinois. Bryan graduated from the University of North Carolina at Chapel Hill in 2005 with degrees in English and Dramatic Art with a minor in Creative Writing.

Bryan has published 28 books and plays. He lives in Chicago.

Made in the USA
San Bernardino, CA
21 December 2015